D0700167

Purgatory

THE CORNELL YEATS

Plays: *The Death of Cuchulain,* edited by Phillip L. Marcus
Purgatory, edited by Sandra F. Siegel

Purgatory

MANUSCRIPT MATERIALS INCLUDING
THE AUTHOR'S FINAL TEXT

BY W. B. YEATS

EDITED BY

SANDRA F. SIEGEL

CORNELL UNIVERSITY PRESS

ITHACA AND LONDON

THIS BOOK HAS BEEN PUBLISHED WITH THE AID OF A GRANT FROM THE HULL MEMORIAL PUBLICATION FUND OF CORNELL UNIVERSITY.

First published 1986 by Cornell University Press.

Library of Congress Cataloging in Publication Data

Yeats, W. B. (William Butler), 1865-1939.
Purgatory : manuscript materials including the author's final text.

(The Cornell Yeats)
1. Yeats, W. B. (William Butler), 1965-1939—Manuscripts—Facsimiles. I. Siegel, Sandra F. II. Title. III. Series: Yeats, W. B. (William Butler), 1865-1939. Works. 1982.
PR5904.P8 1986 822′.8 84-45799
ISBN 0-8014-1802-X (alk. paper)

Printed in the United States of America

The paper in this book is acid-free, and meets the guidelines for permanence and durability of the Committee on Production Guidelines for Book Longevity of the Council on Library Resources.

THE CORNELL YEATS

The volumes in this series will present the manuscripts of W. B. Yeats's poems (all extant versions), plays (complete insofar as possible), and other materials from the rich archives preserved in the collections of Senator Michael B. Yeats, the National Library of Ireland, and elsewhere. The primary goal of the editors is to achieve the greatest possible fidelity in transcription. Some standardization of spacing has been introduced to facilitate typesetting. Photographic facsimiles will be used extensively to supplement the texts.

The series will include some important unpublished works of high literary quality, and individually and as a whole the volumes will help to illuminate Yeats's creative process. They will be essential reference works for scholars who wish to establish definitive texts of the published works. They will contain many passages of biographical interest as well as passages that will be helpful in interpreting other works by Yeats. The emphasis throughout, however, will be on the documents themselves, and critical analysis will be limited to discussion of their significance in relation to the published texts; the editors assume that publication of the documents will stimulate critical studies as a matter of course.

THE YEATS EDITORIAL BOARD

For Jim, Varya, and Susanna

Contents

Preface

Throughout his career Yeats explored the subjects of fathers and sons, pollution and purification, politics and vision. These subjects converge in *Purgatory*. From the time of the first performance of the play, in August 1938, the audiences argued about what Yeats might have intended, what the play might mean, and whether it deserved the highest praise or any praise at all. The performance revived critical debate about belief, art, and morality and provoked fresh questions about whether or not Yeats approved of fascism and believed in ghosts, questions that had vexed readers of his poems and plays earlier in the decade. In the autumn of 1938 questions about Yeats's politics and his theology seemed trivial as the world edged toward catastrophe. But in the world of scholarship debate continued.

The unusual circumstances surrounding the composition and publication of *Purgatory* invite us to consider *Purgatory* and *On the Boiler* as one imaginative unit.[1] The play was to be printed as an epilogue to the essay, and Yeats fully expected that both would reach the public at about the time of the first performance of the play. Despite his efforts to see the manuscript through the press before his death, the printing of *On the Boiler* met with protracted delays. The play was, however, performed as planned, on August 10, as part of the First Abbey Theatre Festival. The first performance stirred a public debate among participants in the festival. For weeks afterward letters were exchanged and editorials were written in the *Irish Times* and *Irish Independent* praising and disparaging the play. Viewers did not deny the play's effectiveness, but they disputed its meaning, as well as its aesthetic worth. They questioned the appropriateness of its performance in a Catholic country, and even suggested that Yeats ought not to have written it. That debate might have been different if *On the Boiler* had reached the public simultaneously. Instead, by the time the pamphlet was published posthumously, interpretations of the play had been formulated. The controversy stirred by the initial performance would be of considerably less interest if, in the history of critical opinion about the play, the initial response had not been, as it still is, rehearsed even by those whose allegiance to Irish politics is remote. Judgments have varied as widely as interpretations; some readers have praised the play as one of Yeats's highest achievements, while others have regarded it with disdain. The manuscript materials presented in this volume will not and cannot resolve all of the interpretive difficulties the play presents, such as whether the Old Man is, as John Health-Stubbs argues, "the revolutionary

[1]*On the Boiler* (italicized) refers to the full text including essay and play; within quotation marks it refers to the title essay.

generation, or Yeats himself,'' or whether *Purgatory* is primarily a political allegory, a ghost play, or simply the tragedy of an old man.[2] They will, however, resolve some of these questions even as they raise new ones about other issues, many of them touched on by Curtis Bradford in *Yeats at Work*. Finally, the manuscripts enable us to see the poet engaged in the exploratory process of crafting the play, of arriving at the final form, and of discovering the lineaments of his convictions—and his doubts. Anthologized more widely than any other of Yeats's plays, and probably performed more frequently, *Purgatory* is his most dramatically intense play. The manuscript materials are characterized by a corresponding intensity: revisions lead to reversals of thought and feeling which, like all reversals, are charged with the drama of discovery.

The earliest drafts reveal the intensity with which Yeats struggled to perfect the play, gradually evolving the same four-beat line he employed in his late poems, and will be of interest to those who admire the sonority of the later Yeats. But the question of Yeats's politics is not negligible. In its most pointed formulation, the issue has been whether or not the Old Man of *Purgatory* is Yeats's own fictional surrogate. Beyond that question is the one of whether Yeats thought violence the only solution to a world that had grown offensive to utopic dreams. Composed and performed on the threshold of the outbreak of the Second World War, the play dramatizes the issue of whether violence can purify pollution or such actions pollute further what they seek to purify. Tracing the history of the revision and publication of *Purgatory* illumines these and other questions that might otherwise remain obscure. The reproduction of the manuscripts is likely to unsettle judgments and provoke fresh interpretations of the play.

On March 15, 1938, Yeats wrote to Edith Shackleton Heald: ''I have a one-act play in my head, a scene of tragic intensity. . . . My recent work has greater strangeness and I think greater intensity than anything I have done. I never remember the dream so deep.''[3] *Purgatory* evolved from his memory of that scene. What differences separate the early version, born of this mood, from the version of the play which emerges from successive revisions? The Introduction that follows addresses this question. Along the way I isolate the patterns of revision in light of the final text and consider the degree to which the manuscripts and the circumstances surrounding their preparation for publication illumine the ultimate version of the play.

The unfailing generosity of Senator Michael B. Yeats and Miss Anne Yeats have made this volume possible. In addition to David R. Clark, Phillip Marcus, and Jon Stallworthy, who have shared with me their wide knowledge of Yeats manuscripts and their editorial wisdom, other persons who have assisted in various ways include Eric Domville, Jacquline Doyle, Richard Ellmann, David Erdman, David Farmer, Sima Godfrey, Narayan Hegde, Kathy Henderson, Maggie Holtzberg, Michael Horniman, John Kelly, Marilan Lund, Donal 'O Luanaigh, John Kirkpatrick, Deirdre McQuillan, Alison Sainsbury, Lyn Scofield, and Elizabeth Swaim. I owe special thanks to Carol Betsch and to the staff of Cornell University Press.

The staffs of the Libraries of Cornell University, the Humanities Research Center, Austin,

[2]John Heath-Stubbs, *The Darkling Plain* (London: Eyre & Spottiswoode, 1950), p. 205.
[3]*The Letters of W. B. Yeats,* ed. Allan Wade (New York: Macmillan, 1955), p. 907.

Texas, the National Library of Ireland, the Sligo County Museum, and Wesleyan University have been unstinting in their help.

I have been assisted by grants from the American Philosophical Society and from Cornell University.

The unpublished material is printed by permission of Michael B. Yeats and Anne Yeats. I am grateful to them and to A. P. Watt and Sons for permission to publish it here, and to David Erdman for permission to reprint material originally published in the *Bulletin of Research in the Humanities*.

S.F.S.

Ithaca, New York

Purgatory

Introduction

The Manuscripts

The manuscripts of *Purgatory* were deposited in the National Library of Ireland by Mrs. William Butler Yeats in October 1957. Eight folders contain the scenario, two manuscript versions of the play, four typescripts, two with corrections in Yeats's hand, and one set of page proofs with Yeats's holograph corrections. These are identified as NLI MSS 8771#1–8. Also in the National Library of Ireland, on the versos of drafts of ''Long-legged Fly,'' are two leaves of manuscript belonging to *Purgatory,* one of which contains prose dialogue and the other a sketch by Yeats of a stage set. These are identified as MS 13,593 (36). Besides these materials, there are one leaf of manuscript from a draft of the play and one set of page proofs corrected in a hand other than Yeats's. Another set of page proofs corrected by Mrs. Yeats is in the British Library and is identified as Add. MS. 58892. One leaf of typescript with corrections in Yeats's hand is among the Cliff House papers in the possession of Senator Michael Yeats. Finally, there is in the Script Room of the Abbey Theatre a printed version of the play which appears to have been used as a prompt copy.

Yeats began to compose the scenario (NLI MS 8771#1) and two holograph verse drafts (NLI MSS 8771#2 and #3) of the play in late March and probably completed them in manuscript the latter part of April 1938, although he continued to make revisions on the typescripts, the last one of which was probably prepared during May. Internal evidence indicates that after writing the scenario he began to compose the first verse draft (MS 8771#2). Although he revised heavily, he established, almost immediately, the same four-beat line in which he had cast *The Herne's Egg* and ''Under Ben Bulben.'' In the second verse draft (MS 8771#3) he perfected the metrical frame, was more attentive to stage directions, and arrived at a version from which a typescript could be prepared. Although he composed swiftly and over a brief period of time, the manuscripts reveal distinct patterns of revision which separate the final version from the early drafts.

Although there is insufficient evidence to determine exactly when Yeats completed the scenario or either one of the verse drafts, he probably composed *Purgatory* in three successive stages beginning with the scenario, and proceeding to the first, and then to the second, verse version. Having begun to compose in the latter part of March 1938, he wrote on April 6 of being ''in the middle of my one act play,'' and on May 3 of wanting ''three or four more days to finish my play.''[1] Yeats entrusted the typescript to F. R. Higgins to give to a printer; since Higgins, who had been on tour in America with the Abbey Theatre Company did not return until the end of June, it could not have reached the printer before then. It is likely, though, that during May, after Yeats completed *Purgatory,* either Mrs. Yeats or a typist prepared the clean typescript, probably from a previously prepared typescript on some pages of which Yeats had introduced revisions. That typescript may well have been ready a week or two before he actually gave it to Higgins, toward the end of June, when he returned to Dublin. On June 16, 1938, Yeats wrote that he expected *On the Boiler* would be ''published in about a month,'' and on December 23, 1938, he wrote of it having gone to the printer ''seven months ago.''[2]

It is not possible to know over how many hours Yeats composed or on how many occasions. Bradford, on the strength of Yeats's having written approximately one third of the scenario in pencil and the first and last thirds in ink, reasonably concludes that Yeats composed in at least two sittings, but in the absence of more substantial evidence it is impossible to be certain.[3] Of considerably greater interest, however, are the discernible patterns of revision that characterize the three distinct stages of composition.

Patterns of Revision

In the scenario Yeats sketched the plot of *Purgatory.* In MS 8771#2 and MS 8771#3, he retained the same sequence: the return of the Old Man and his son to the ruined house; the dispute between them over whether the ghosts are real or imagined; the Old Man's description of the dead who relive the moments of crisis in their lives; the recounting of the history of the house; the ghosts' reenactment of their marriage night; the Boy's theft; the Old Man's threat; the rehearsal of the murder of the Old Man's father; the murder of the Boy; and the return of the beating hooves. The scenario, however, contains more than the plot. The place to which the Old Man and his son return—the ancestral house that is the scene of the marriage night of the Old Man's parents—is described as being an evil place; the Old Man thinks of himself as being under a curse, and is determined to put his mother's soul to rest, although he is uncertain how to accomplish this. He describes the horses' beating hooves as her thought, and as her thought alone. How much knowledge of her transgressions the mother has before her marriage, at the time of her death in childbirth, and, after her death, as time passes, as a shade, are questions that remain to be clarified.

The conclusion of the scenario contains the core of two distinct motives that Yeats

[1]Letters to ''Dobbs'' [Mrs. Yeats], April 6 and May 3, 1938. Hitherto unpublished letters are forthcoming in *The Collected Letters of W. B. Yeats,* ed. John Kelly (Oxford: Oxford University Press). Unpublished letters cited below whose locations are not indicated were made available to me by Eric Domville.

[2]*Letters,* ed. Wade, pp. 910 and 921. On July 13, Yeats wrote of having given the manuscript to F. R. Higgins to send to the printer before he left Dublin. Yeats had left Dublin by July 13. Ibid., p. 912. On July 1, 1938, the *Irish Times* correspondent reported having ''met Mr. F. R. Higgins after his strenuous tour with the Abbey Theatre Company. . . . The nine months' travelling across the United States was an experience, but he was glad to get home.''

[3]Curtis B. Bradford, *Yeats at Work* (Carbondale: Southern Illinois University Press, 1965), p. 295.

disentangled from each other only in subsequent revisions: one is whether or not the mother does ''know all'' and, if she does, what difference her knowledge makes to her suffering. The second is whether or not the Old Man, in murdering his son, has ''finished the evil'' that the mother's marriage set in motion. When Yeats revised the scenario on the verso of its second page, introducing the word ''transgressions,'' he opened the possibilities that became, in later versions, a means of accounting for the suffering of the mother as a result not merely of the evil she set in motion but also of the transgressions she committed against herself, or her soul. The complexity of the play's ''theology''—by which I mean the way in which the relation between evil and knowledge is understood either by Yeats or by the Old Man—increased rather than decreased with successive revisions, particularly as it bears on the figure of the Old Man. Yeats shaped and reshaped the Old Man, who in the scenario thinks of himself as evil, as the pollutant. In the final version of the play there is no trace left of Yeats's having initially cast him in this role. Instead, he is presented as a man who thinks of himself as a savior.

In the scenario, and in the early stages of revision (MS 8771#2), the Old Man identifies himself with his father even as he identifies his son with himself as being evil. Through his successive revisions, the last of which occurs on pages $VB7^r$ and $VB8^r$ of MS 8771#3, Yeats deleted all references to the father who murdered the house and all of the Old Man's references to his father, himself, and his son as being evil: instead, Yeats fixes the Old Man's attention on the fall of the great ancestral house.[4] The most striking revisions of the scenario made in the first verse draft have the effect of gradually decreasing the Old Man's sense of himself as an evil and accursed pollutant and of increasing, at the same time, the confidence of his tone. Finally, as Yeats revised the second verse draft he deleted almost entirely the Old Man's disparaging allusions to himself. These deletions contribute, in large measure, to the shaping of a figure who is a self-declared moralist. Although Yeats deliberately and consistently eliminated the Old Man's view of himself as evil, he did not alter the Old Man's behavior from one version to the next. He did modify details of the scene of the murder of the father as he began to revise MS 8771#3. These revisions, which emphasize how pointed the Old Man's actions are, also heighten his ignorance.

In the scenario the Old Man narrates how he strangled his father in the burning house. This account is unchanged in MS 8771#2. In MS 8771#3, however, Yeats revised that scene and ultimately retained some of those revisions. It is conceivable that when he began to compose the play he had in mind the Sphinx of the Oedipus legend who strangles its victims. Whatever the origin, he gradually eliminated all references in the play to death by strangulation and introduced the knife as the weapon of violence.

The revisions of the Old Man's account of the murder of his father required parallel revisions of the murder of the son. In the scenario the Boy is more provocative and the Old Man more deliberate. In subsequent versions Yeats so reduced the Boy's provocation that neither his theft of the money from the pack nor any other obvious cause can explain the Old Man's precipitous murder. In the second verse version, the actual murder of the Boy is as spontaneous and uncontrolled an act of passion and anger as the murder of the Old Man's father had been. It is provoked by the Old Man's vision of his mother's marriage night rather

[4]The system of notation is explained on p. 30.

than by the Boy's threats. The fictional Old Man became increasingly complex as Yeats continued to revise the version. In the earliest versions the Old Man is shrewdly accurate about himself. As the Boy's provocative behavior and the Old Man's sense of himself as evil are gradually pruned away, the revisions served to emphasize the confusion within the Old Man. As a result, the motives that prompt him to act appear to be at odds with his verbal account of his behavior.

The sequence that follows the Old Man's discovery of the Boy's attempted theft is altered only slightly in MS 8771#2. The changes from the scenario to the first verse version are not very great, either, but they are of interest. We can see how Yeats transformed the scenario in the process of casting his conception dramatically. In this earliest version the Old Man is boldly decisive. He understands that he brought his son to the house to kill him, to terminate the lineage. When the Boy resists, the Old Man throws him down and describes how he strangled his own father and abandoned him in the burning house. The Boy, who sees the ghosts of the Old Man's mother and father for the first time, interrupts the narrative. The Old Man's line, as he summons the Boy—"that I may kill & my mother find rest know that the evil is finished"—is followed by a provisional stage direction, placed in parenthesis: "(boy rises & comes slowly to the Old—who strangles him)." The Boy submits to the authority of his father and willingly offers himself as though in ritual sacrifice. In the succeeding versions, beginning with the first verse version, Yeats adjusted the relation of the Old Man and the Boy to each other somewhat differently. Yeats arrived, or nearly arrived, at the final version of the pivotal scene in the typescript marked "A" (MS 8771#5), on which he made further holograph revisions. While the Old Man's motives are clear in earlier versions, the holograph addition blurs them. He murders his son neither to purify the house, nor to save his mother's soul, nor to terminate the lineage polluted by an evil curse, although in retrospect these might have been construed by the Old Man to have been his motives. With the holograph addition, TS5 suggests a more complex and precarious intent: the actual reappearance of his mother displaces his imaginings about the agony she suffers in reliving her dream. He is transfixed by the vision before him as though it were *his* dream, one that recurs repeatedly in spite of his efforts to free himself from it. The murder of his son occurs as though it were the murder of the father once again.

Of the scene in which the Old Man presents his view of the dead, Yeats made only minor revisions. In the sequence of variants that unfold, from the scenario to the page proofs corrected in his hand, the revisions of this scene consist largely of replacing with a more abstract austerity the excess of passion and intensity which characterized the Old Man's language. In the scenario the Old Man describes the dead who return to the places of their transgressions to live over and over again the moments when their life came to a crisis. On page 3 of MS 8771#2, Yeats expanded this description of what happens to the soul in purgatory. In MS 8771#2 the Old Man amplifies the distinction he draws between the suffering of the dead that can and the suffering that cannot be affected by the living. In the second verse draft the Old Man recognizes that the dead recurrently relive their past.

Yeats concluded the scenario with a set of questions, at least one of which—"Oh my God what is man"—recalls a Sophoclean chorus, the riddling Sphinx, and Oedipus who saved the city by answering the riddle yet is himself the cause of pollution. In subsequent versions of

Purgatory, rather than pose this question so directly, the Old Man explored and resolved other questions—Can the soul of his mother hear him? Does it see all? Does it understand that the evil it set in motion is finished? Are the misery of the living and the remorse of the dead unending?—that recur frequently in the first draft version of the play, usually as intrusions that Yeats eventually decided to delete. At times the dynastic theme is prominent, while at others the mother's transgression against herself preempts our attention. In the last lines of the scenario the two themes are fused. The conception of the dead reliving moments of crisis is clarified in later versions, but only insofar as it interlocks with the theme of the great house.

Precisely how much knowledge the mother's spirit has is the subject of considerable revision. According to the view the Old Man propounds in the revisions in MS 8771#2 (p. 5^{r}) and MS 8771#3 (pp. 4^{r}, 3^{v}, and 5^{r}), the dead, who have full knowledge of hindsight as the living do not, also "know all." We take for granted that the mother's knowledge is complete largely because Yeats brings her into focus through the eyes of the Old Man. Once having identified the Old Man and the mother, Yeats was bound to take up, in some dramatic form, the question of whether the living could intervene on behalf of the dead. Although the answer is clear, the Old Man is driven by the strength of his desire to actions that conflict with his convictions. Yeats made similar revisions of the passages that turn on the question of what the Old Man and the mother know about themselves. In revising, for example, on page 9^{r}, MS 8771#2, and page 8^{r}, MS 8771#3, but also on pages 13^{v}–14^{r}, MS 8771#2, and page 7^{v}, MS 8771#3, entire passages are deleted in which the Old Man explains why his actions will make no difference to his mother's suffering. The effect of these excisions is to heighten the dramatic efficacy of the Old Man's prayer of the last lines of the play, even as they make more plausible the continued efforts to intervene to save her. Yeats retained, nevertheless, the Old Man's characteristic attitude and tone: his mother is "locked in her own dream"; "nothing can be changed"; events are irreversible. These are the apprehensions of a man who desperately wants to intervene on his mother's behalf, although everything he understands about the world ought to lead him to see that he cannot alter the course of events as they have happened and as they will happen.

Yeats eventually excised passages about the mother's soul from the Old Man's speeches. He did not retain the line "She does not care if I see it / in the eye of the mind" or any other significant passages in which the Old Man describes himself as evil or as the pollution. He also excised the metaphor that describes the soul as being locked in its dream, reducing that lengthy passage to

if I should throw
A stick or a stone they would not hear
And that s a proof my wits are out [MS 8771#3, 7^{v}, ll. 5–7]

The questions of whether or not the soul in purgatory can apprehend the earthly world and those still earthbound can affect the lives of spirits culminate in both verse drafts as the problem of whether or not the pleasure of the sexual act is renewed, although this is precisely the act that represents the transgression. Peter Ure, in his incisive essay on the play, has noted that the latter point "is as pretty an entanglement as Yeats ever devised."[5] Earlier versions of this passage, one of which occurs in MS 8771#2, and which is given below, are substantively similar to later revisions, although the later versions are more austere:

And hear a problem boy
She
~~Resolve this proble~~m boy— ~~They~~ lives
Through everything in exact detail
~~But does she live in in her thought alone~~
~~But is that only in her thought, or~~ is
But is that in her thought alone or is
~~The pleasure of the sexual act renewed~~
~~to it by su~~ Compelled to it by suffering & yet
~~Compelled by suffering, and yet~~ ~~Compelled to it by remorse~~
relive
Can she renew the sexual act
~~Without some pleasure in it~~
And find no pleasure it & if not
If suffering & pleasure must be there
Which is then greater~~—& heres a thought theres~~ a problem
~~That needs Tur~~ Go ~~f~~ fetch Turtullian boy
For I have it solved upon the instant
While they are begetting me [MS 8771#2, 11^{r}, ll. 1–16]

This passage from the first verse version anticipates the last scene of the second verse draft. However, the last scene of the first verse draft differs significantly from the final version of the second. In the last scene of the final version of the first verse draft the Old Man, shortly after he describes what he sees in the window, murders the Boy:

Old Man
He has come to the front room to find [~~?the~~] a gla
A tired beast [~~?and~~] Where did I read these words
Then the bride sleep fell upon ~~Adam~~ Adam
is
Yet there nothing in the window nothing
But the impression upon my mothers mind
She is alone in her remorse
That tired beast there knowing nothing
If I should kill a man under the window
He would not even turn his head, [MS 8771#2, 13^{r}, ll. 1–9]

The survival from earlier revisions of the tone of alarm is odd. In the first verse draft the

[5]Peter Ure, *Yeats the Playwright* (New York: Barnes and Noble, 1963), p. 107.

Old Man recognizes that the living and the dead are severed from one another; in the later revisions it is as though he were testing his perception of that situation. The intensity with which the Old Man grasps that the living cannot affect the dead is equaled by the intensity of his desire to intervene. Moreover, his response to his son is prompted by the anguish provoked by seeing his mother, "locked into her dream," reenacting the sexual act. In the first version of this scene in MS 8771#2, the emphasis falls on the mother's inability to apprehend the earthly consequences of her actions; in the last revision of the first version, it falls on the Old Man's justification for having murdered his son:

Dear mother
Because I have finished all that evil
The window empty sink into your peace
I killed that lad because he had youth
And soon would take some woman s fancy
~~And he pass the blood polution~~ on
And so pass the polution on
{B
{but I am a wretched foul old man [MS 8771#2, 13^{r}, ll. 21–24, MS 8771#2, 14^{r}, ll. 1–4]

In the earliest revisions of the first verse version the Old Man tries to account for the return, after the murder, of the beating of the hooves. Yeats wrote and then cancelled the following passage:

That distant sound—~~hor [?]~~ that the horse hoof means
That she relives her marriage ~~that~~ night
an
Not because of outward consequences
That man can end but because
Of what has happened in her soul [MS 8771#2, 13^{v}, ll. 1–5]

He tried again, but cancelled the lines before he had got very far:

Until the dead tramp killed in a brawl
~~Horse hoove~~—
That sound again—horse hoofs again [MS 8771#2, 13^{v}, ll. 6–8]

He proceeded to sketch the passage he later expanded and strengthened:

~~her past~~
from ~~her vision~~ the
O God release my mother ~~from her dream~~ from ~~her~~ vision
For I can do no more ~~le relea~~ appease
The misery of the living the remorse of the dead [MS 8771#2, 14^{r}, ll. 12–14]

As the Old Man is brought to the recognition that he can do nothing more than he has already done, he appeals to God. It is worthy of notice that at this latest stage of revision, Yeats omitted the reasons that the Old Man had presented earlier for the soul's reliving of its past. Finally, in other lines, in revising further, he joined together a passage that supplies the reasons for the soul's punishment to the passage that includes his prayer. Bringing both passages within the compass of a single speech, Yeats transformed the Old Man's simple recognition that he "can do no more" to the more deeply disturbing awareness that, because the mother's suffering is caused by her transgression against herself, what he had done did not and could not have helped her.

> Because of what her marriage did to her self
>   not to others but to her own soul
> To ~~her own soul~~ & what I think
> And what I did is but vain
> O God release my mothers soul
>   mankind
> There s nothing∧~~I~~ can do [?] appease
> The misery of the living the remorse of the dead [MS 8771#2, 13^{v}, ll. 15–20]

In his last revision in this first verse version of the play Yeats omitted once again the account of why the soul of the mother must relive the marriage night and emphasized again the sense of recurrence that arouses the Old Man's anguish. Yeats's revision of the Old Man's "I" to "mankind" shifted his recognition that "there s nothing mankind can do [?] appease / The misery of the living and the remorse of the dead" from a personal to an impersonal predicament.

> Hoof beats, hoof beats,
>   hoof
> ~~That distant sound~~—those ~~horse~~ beats mean
> That she must animate that dead night
>   and
> Again∧again ~~& yet again on—on~~ on, on, on, on
> O God release my mother s soul
> Theres nothing mankind can do appease
> The misery of the living & the remorse of the dead [MS 8771#2, 14^{r}, ll. 15–21]

Yeats continued to revise in the second verse version of the play. Only at this relatively late stage of composition did he discover the dramatic potential of reintroducing the thunder-blasted tree, creating a plangent theatrical pause between the murder of the boy and the sound of the hooves. He refined, as well, the final passages. The figure of the tree as the purified soul was one of the latest additions he made. Its effect depends in large part upon the expectation—which proves to be false—that the dream will not return. He continued to revise the passage he had fashioned in the first verse version in MS 8771#3:

beats
Hoof∧—Hoof beat~~—that dream returns;~~
it & I
Her mind cannot ~~prefe~~ prevent ~~that dream returning~~
And I am ~~and~~
[? ? ?]∧tw twice a murderer∧for nothing.
And she must animate that dead night
~~Again again~~ again & yet again Not once but many times; O God
[MS 8771#3, 12^{r}, ll. 10–14]

As he revised further, the only significant change is one of tone:

Hoof beats— O my God hoof beats
How quickly it returns; beat; beat
~~Her mind cannot prevent that dream retu~~
Her mind cannot hold up that dream
Twice a murderer & for nothing
And she must animate that dead night
Not once but many times. O God [MS 8771#3, 11^{v}, ll. 5–11]

He then concluded with the same prayer:

{R
~~O God~~ {release my mother s soul from its dream;
no more
~~There's nothing~~ Mankind can do,∧appease
The misery of the living and the remorse of the dead [MS 8771#3, 12^{r}, ll. 15–17]

Two similar situations are joined, each of which gains in dramatic effectiveness because of the other: the Old Man who reenacts his violence resembles shades who repeatedly relive their memories. Both the living and the dead are driven by intense desires that prompt actions the consequences of which are greater than they can comprehend or control. The revisions allow us to see how carefully Yeats crafted the contrast between the Old Man's reasoning on the one side and, on the other, the grotesque drama he enacts. Yeats brings the Old Man to a full stop on the threshold of the recognition that he is "twice a murderer and all for nothing." As this stunning line diverts the attention of the audience from the world of spirits and rivets it on the living, so the Old Man is diverted from his concern with purification. He is consumed by the thought that neither he nor anyone else can make a difference to the suffering of the dead.

The awesome intensity of the last scene derives from the swift reversals of thought and feeling within the Old Man: the sound of the beating hooves transforms his hope into the horror of his recognition of his failure successfully to intervene. In a certain sense, the only sense that really matters to the man, the murders were for nothing because the marriage night will continue to haunt him. And yet, if he were to acknowledge his failure, he would be obliged to repudiate his arguments. At precisely the moment when his failure ought to summon the dynastic theme or, as one might expect, his sense of his mother's anguish, he invokes neither one. Even as he appears to see himself, a queer blindness blurs his acuity. He remains ignorant that he is the pollution as he remains ignorant that the two murders have been in vain for reasons other than those he recognizes.

The hooves return for two reasons, neither one of which the Old Man understands: his mother's soul will not rest as long as he survives or as long as the spirit is compelled to reenact her transgression against herself. Why did the Old Man imagine that his mother's soul would be at peace after he murdered father and son, if he knew she must suffer for her own transgression? And why, after realizing that his mother's own transgression causes her to relive the marriage night, did the Old Man think that ending the consequence upon others was "for nothing"? Peter Ure points out that there are things "the old man 'knows' and does not *know,* and what he does not *know,* or does not fully understand, is an important element in his tragedy." What the Old Man knows is "the nature of the mother's self-degradation, the consequences that she commits upon herself; but he does not understand it himself." The Old Man "is unable to relate what is happening with what as a character inside the play's action he does not *know,* namely, that the dead

> know at last
> The consequences of those transgressions
> Whether upon others or upon themselves . . .
> upon themselves,
> There is no help but in themselves
> And in the mercy of God."

Having assigned two voices to the Old Man, Ure is obliged to attribute some of the lines to the Old Man as though he were a character inside the play, while attributing other lines to him as though he were not. The Old Man's double role explains his inability to "collate his two kinds of knowledge." Ure's formulation is important enough to quote at length: "If he were able to collate his two kinds of knowledge, which being in a state of crazy half-knowledge, he is not, he would know his mother's condition to its depths; he would not suppose that the killing of the boy could do more than momentarily assuage her torment. This state of half-knowledge is his hereditary condition entailed upon him by his polluted blood. It is his tragic fate."[6]

Yeats's revisions of the manuscript materials invite consideration of at least two further observations that bear on the Old Man's knowledge. Ure, who relied primarily on the printed text, might have been led to modify his argument in light of the manuscript materials. As Yeats presents the Old Man in the final version, his moral rage, so strongly directed in the first half of the play toward the purification of the great house, subsides in the second half as his lust is directed toward his mother. The themes interlock as though to account for and provoke one another. His desire, which he acts upon, to purge the ancestral house, conflicts

[6]Ibid., pp. 109–110.

with his desire to bring his mother's soul to rest. (He cannot see himself as the pollution so long as he sees himself as the savior.) He acts as though he alone can make a difference, although until the soul helps itself nothing he does can alter its situation. This is a question neither of half-knowledge nor of fate. Yeats dramatizes two conflicting impulses in the Old Man, who understands both but fails to recognize that they conflict with each other. The Old Man's failure to understand the conditions of souls in purgatory is the result of the presence of a power that obfuscates his understanding.

Although it would not have been possible to draw this conclusion from earlier versions of the play, in retrospect it appears as though the revisions were guided by a coherent conception that prefigured the final version. The "scene of tragic intensity" that Yeats envisioned before he began to compose undoubtedly differed from the scene he dramatized. In the process of recasting his vision, he crafted a play that has the intensity of a dream. When he wrote, on March 15, 1938, of his recent work's having greater intensity than anything he had done and of never having remembered "the dream so deep," he must surely have had in mind the scene that was to evolve into *Purgatory*. He did not describe the details of the original scene, but of this much we can be certain: as he transformed that scene, he shaped a figure whose awareness of how abominable he is steadily decreased as Yeats himself gained greater control, insight, and distance from his subject.

If we were to read the final version as showing Yeats's approval of the Old Man, depending on how we read "On the Boiler" we might find support there for that approval: when he wrote in the prefatory note to *On the Boiler* that he had included other writings that were related thematically, Yeats invited readers to link them. We know that after he had sketched "On the Boiler" he began to write the play. In the process of revising the play, he continued to revise the essay. Those revisions, of the play but also of the essay, seem to have had the effect of modifying the argument he proposed in early drafts of both. If Yeats had revised neither the play nor the essay, it would probably be fair to say that *Purgatory* is the animation of his conservative beliefs about eugenic reform. The final versions of *Purgatory* and "On the Boiler," however, allow for a different reading.

During the weeks when Yeats was composing both, he persisted in imagining play and essay as a single unit. To the extent that *Purgatory* is an essential part of the design and argument of "On the Boiler," the essay and play are inseparable. Yeats decided to append *Purgatory* to "On the Boiler" probably sometime after he began to compose the play, certainly before he completed his revisions of the essay. Once having decided to augment the essay, he then prepared the preface, in which he wrote that the poems and play he included were related to his main theme. He added several other transitional passages, some of which reiterate his skeptical attitude toward his own thought. It is possible that he had not yet conceived of augmenting the essay as he wrote the scenario and first version of the play. Nevertheless, the Old Man who describes himself in the scenario and first version as "accursed" and "evil" is as preoccupied with purification as Yeats is in the essay. But in the final stage of composition, as Yeats brings his fictional hero more fully to life, the Old Man loses almost entirely the self-knowledge he possesses in earlier versions. He is no less preoccupied with purification than in earlier versions: on the contrary, as he grows increasingly ignorant that he is the pollution, he is more intensely preoccupied with purification—and more powerless. We can only speculate as to whether the reception of the play, which is the dramatization of that dilemma, might have been different if it had been read before it was performed and reached the public, as Yeats intended and expected it would, in the *On the Boiler* edition. But neither Yeats's intentions nor his expectations were fulfilled. *Purgatory* was performed on at least six occasions before it was published, and it was first published not as the epilogue to the essay but in *Last Poems and Two Plays.*[7]

The Publication of *On the Boiler*

The printing of the typescript of *On the Boiler,* which Yeats gave to F. R. Higgins in late June 1938, met with protracted delays at the printer over the next seven months. Shortly before Yeats's death in January 1939 he prepared the table of contents for *Last Poems and Two Plays,* which was published in June 1939. But it is the manuscript of *Purgatory* in the *On the Boiler* edition, over which edition Yeats had labored extensively, which is of greater interest. Of this edition there were two printings: one by the inexperienced Longford Press, and the other by Alex. Thom & Company. Between April and June 1938, Yeats adjusted passages of the essay and play to form a single imaginative unit and made holograph corrections on the typescripts; he corrected the galleys prepared by the Longford Press in the autumn of that year; and, by January 10, 1939, he had corrected the page proofs prepared from the corrected galleys.[8] He returned the corrected page proofs to Dublin from the South of France and requested a second set that incorporated his revisions. If Yeats sent the proofs by airmail, it is possible that they reached Longford within three days. (Ordinarily one would allow for two weeks from the South of France to Dublin.)[9] Even if the printer set to work at once, which would have been unlikely, the second set of proofs could not have reached Yeats before he was overcome by illness several days before he died on January 28. Yeats, then, did not see the second set of page proofs from which the Longford Press printed five hundred copies, all but four of which were destroyed according to Mrs. Yeats's wishes.[10] Probably it was Mrs. Yeats who engaged Alex. Thom & Company to print a new edition. The latter printing, which could only have been prepared after the poet's death, is less authoritative than the Longford printing Yeats himself saw to press. But the Longford rather than the Alex. Thom printing holds our interest for at least one other equally compelling reason.

Yeats's writing of *Purgatory* was so fused with the composition of "On the Boiler," and the printing of the two so inextricably linked, that it is impossible to consider the history of one without considering the history of the other. Their publication is more difficult to trace than their composition, the one in relation to the other, partly because Yeats did not live to see the volume through the press and partly because his plans for the publication of the volume were bound so closely to his plans for the first, and then the second and third,

[7]See Curtis Bradford's discussion of the text, "On Yeats's *Last Poems,*" in *Yeats, Last Poems: A Casebook,* ed. Jon Stallworthy (London: Macmillan, 1968), pp. 75–97.

[8]See letter to the Longford Printing Press, January 10, 1939, Cliff House, Dalkey, Republic of Ireland.

[9]See *Irish Times,* February 3, 1939.

[10]See Allan Wade, *A Bibliography of the Writings of W. B. Yeats,* 3d ed. rev. and edited by Russell K. Alspach (London: Rupert Hart-Davis, 1968), p. 201.

performance of the play. Behind his interest in having the essay and play reach the public simultaneously lay his concern about their reception. A history of their publication must consider how he imagined *Purgatory* and "On the Boiler" might have been read and received if his plans for the publication of the pamphlet had not met with unforseen obstacles.

After having envisioned a "scene of tragic intensity" about which he wrote to Edith Shackleton Heald on March 15, 1938, Yeats composed swiftly. On April 6 he wrote of being "in the middle" of his new play and by May he thought it nearly complete.[11] By May 3, 1938, he had decided to yoke play and essay together, writing to Mrs. Yeats: "I want if possible three or four more days to finish my play and three short new sections for *On the Boiler.*"[12] He had not planned to augment the essay when he conceived the play nor in late March when he began to compose the play. As he proceeded, a volume began to emerge which differed considerably from the one he had in mind.

Yeats had planned *On the Boiler* in November 1937 as a casual miscellany. Once he had begun to compose in December 1937, his initial plans gave way to the argument he eventually evolved after considerable revision.[13] A letter to Dorothy Wellesley contains his first mention of the pamphlet. He was concerned about its effect:

> I shall be busy writing a *Fors Clavigera* of sorts—my advice to the youthful mind on all manner of things, and poems. After going into accounts I find that I can make Cuala prosperous if I write this periodical and publish it bi-annually. It will be an amusing thing to do—I shall curse my enemies and bless my friends. My enemies will hit back, and that will give me the joy of answering them.[14]

At this point Yeats was probably more concerned with the survival of the press than with its prosperity. The precise causes of Cuala's financial difficulties remain obscure, but his fear that the bank would carry out its threatened foreclosure on his sister Lolly's Sligo shares unless the press paid its outstanding debts is evident in his letters. On December 18, 1937, he wrote that although he "knew nothing of the present financial crisis of the firm until a few weeks ago," he would remedy the situation by taking matters into his own hands and reorganizing the Cuala.[15] By January 4, 1938, he had informed himself of the accounts, arrived at an agreement with Mr. Scroops, the banker, instructed Lolly how to manage the accounts in the future, and advised her to keep him informed through bi-weekly letters. On this date he wrote to Lolly:

> At the end of December the money due to you on the sale of BROADSIDES and

[11] *Letters,* ed. Wade, p. 907, and letter to "Dobbs" (Mrs. Yeats), April 6, 1938.

[12] Letter to Mrs. Yeats, May 3, 1938.

[13] For a fuller discussion of this, see Bradford, *Yeats at Work,* chaps. 10 and 12, and my article "Yeats's Quarrel with Himself: The Design and Argument of Yeats's *On the Boiler,*" *Bulletin of Research in the Humanities,* 21 (1978): 349–368.

[14] *Letters,* ed. Wade, p. 900.

[15] Letter to Lolly Yeats, December 18, 1937.

> ESSAYS amounted to £239. This with money due to you on cards etc should be enough to run the business until April. Should however any temporary hitch arise you must communicate with George; I have made arrangements to meet the difficulty. (I shall be on my way to the S. of France when you get this.)[16]

Yeats's plan for writing *On the Boiler* and his concern with the solvency of the press were inseparable. The Cuala was still on his mind when he wrote to Lily, his other sister: "I have finished the first number and put in a note on your Diana Murphy embroideries. Some rich American may buy the lot."[17] He expected that the press would begin to incur new debts in April but believed that *On the Boiler* would soon be published and yield sufficient income to enable the Cuala Press to pay some of its creditors. "All my immediate plans for Cuala," he wrote to Mrs. Yeats on April 26, 1938, "depend on *On the Boiler*. It can be sent for review and I am preparing publicity for it but it should come out as soon as can be managed."[18] This might have happened promptly if he had not decided to add *Purgatory* as an epilogue to the essay. The performance of the play at the First Abbey Theatre Festival in August 1938 presented him with an opportunity to increase the sales of the pamphlet.[19]

While it is clear that Yeats had the income of the press in mind, it is equally clear from the manuscripts of "On the Boiler" that he composed the essay and arranged the text neither casually nor hastily. As there were some things a man must not do to save a nation (a phrase of John O'Leary's which Yeats frequently repeated), so it would have been uncharacteristic of him to have compromised his art to save Cuala. Moreover, his interest in the press may well have revived in him an old controversy about the fidelity of the artist to the "play of the mind."[20] Some readers, bewildered by the odd title, have thought of the essay as a "potboiler" and mistakenly supposed "On the Boiler" was written as a salable miscellany. The title, though, refers to an actual steamship boiler that served as a podium for mad McCoy, a man whom Yeats had encountered as a boy and who would speak at length on whatever topic came to mind. Yeats mentions this in the essay; he is more explicit in one of his letters: "I have all but finished the first number of my political publication. I call it 'on the boiler' in commemoration of a mad ship's carpenter who, in my childhood, used to preach from the top of an old steamship boiler on the Sligo keys."[21]

Yeats spoke of his own "*Fors Clavigera* of sorts" in order to suggest a publication that, like Ruskin's of that title, would be serial. Unlike Ruskin, who had hoped to educate and

[16]Letter to Lolly Yeats, January 4, 1938.

[17]Letter to Lily Yeats, March 3, 1938.

[18]Letter to "Dobbs" (Mrs. Yeats), April 26, 1938.

[19]On April 26, 1938 (datable from internal evidence) he wrote to Lolly that he had written *On the Boiler* "especially to advertise Cuala. . . . I expect much notice in the press & a quick sale: I spent two months on it while in France. It is now completely finished and typed." But to Mrs. Yeats he wrote on May 3: "I want three or four more days to finish my play & three short new sections for *On the Boiler*. . . . I may have a compromise of an acceptable nature to propose about *Player Queen*. There will be too my new play." The issue that called for compromise is not clear, but it most certainly involved offering his new play, which was linked with his plans for the Cuala and the sale of *On the Boiler*. Although *The Player Queen* was not performed during the two-week festival, *Cathleen Ni Houlihan* and *On Baile's Strand* were.

[20]See, for example, *The Autobiography of William Butler Yeats* (New York: Collier, 1967), p. 218.

[21]In the published text, see *On the Boiler*, p. 9; the passage I cite is from a letter to Ethel Mannin dated January 24, 1938, among the Yeats papers in the Sligo County Library and Museum.

persuade members of Saint George's Guild of the value of their communal experiment, Yeats addressed a wide and diverse audience.[22] On December 17, 1937, he wrote to Dorothy Wellesley: "For the first time in my life I am saying what are my political beliefs." And on the same day, he wrote Ethel Mannin: "I have never discussed with you my political opinions; . . . indeed I have never discussed them with anybody."[23] Letters Yeats wrote between December 1937 and January 1939, the draft of that part of the essay he completed by January 4, 1938, and the revisions he made between January and July 1938 confirm that, as he augmented the essay with several poems and a play, the design and argument of *On the Boiler* grew more complex.[24] By May 3, when he thought the play nearly complete, he had brought the essay and play under one title. Moreover, when he submitted the play to the Abbey board sometime before June 16, he was already anticipating the August festival, the manuscript of *On the Boiler* had been completed, and he expected it to be published in about a month.[25] If plans had gone smoothly, the text of *On the Boiler* would have reached the public shortly before or after the performance of *Purgatory,* but actual publication was delayed probably because F. R. Higgins, to whom Yeats had given the manuscript, "in pure eccentricity" according to Yeats, had chosen an inept and inexperienced printer.[26]

By September 4, 1938, Yeats believed that *On the Boiler* had gone to press, and by November 4 with new plans for a second performance of *Purgatory* underway, he wrote to Higgins: "I forgot to say please worry the Longford people so that *On the Boiler* may be out when my play is performed. I have not yet had the paged proofs." On November 22, Yeats wrote to Higgins asking him to "get Eric Gorman to send him any press notices of his *Purgatory* revival." Announcements appeared in the *Irish Times* on Saturday, December 3, and ran for the week of December 5–10. Anticipating another performance of the play, probably after the New Year, he wrote to Higgins on December 24, 1938: "I want *Purgatory* played from 'On the Boiler' version and the text in the hands of the public as soon as possible after the performance." He continued to hope that the long-awaited edition would finally go to press.[27] But further complications delayed publication beyond yet another performance at the Arts Theatre of Cambridge, where the Abbey Theatre Company of Dublin performed the

[22]Donald T. Torchiana's suggestion, presumably based on the letter of November 11, 1937, to Dorothy Wellesley, that "Yeats's admitted antecedent was Ruskin's *Fors Clavigera,*" is in some need of clarification. Ruskin's *Fors* is an antecedent for Yeats's *On the Boiler* insofar as Yeats imagined a continuing enterprise and in Yeats's expectation, before he began to compose, that he would proffer "advice to the youthful mind"; Torchiana, *W. B. Yeats and Georgian Ireland* (Evanston: Northwestern University Press, 1966), p. 340. I see no evidence to suggest that Yeats shared Ruskin's beliefs, understood his carefully chosen acronymic title, or was attentive to the richness of the metonymic complexity of his "miscellany," in contrast, for example, to Ezra Pound, whose *Cantos* are far more deeply influenced by Ruskin's *Fors.* Nevertheless, Yeats must surely have recognized in the late Ruskin a "yearning . . . for a cleansing and reordering of civilization" resembling his own, and, for that reason, been drawn to the *Fors.* See Guy Davenport, "The House That Jack Built," in *The Geography of the Imagination* (San Francisco: North Point Press, 1981), p. 46.

[23]*Letters,* ed. Wade, pp. 902–903.

[24]See Bradford, *Yeats at Work,* pp. 377–385.

[25]See *Letters,* ed. Wade, p. 910.

[26]See letter to Ethel Mannin, December 23, 1938, in *Letters,* ed. Wade, p. 921.

[27]Letter to F. R. Higgins, December 24, 1938, Humanities Research Center, University of Texas at Austin. See letter to Edith Shackleton Heald, September 4, 1938, in *Letters,* ed. Wade, p. 915, and letters to F. R. Higgins, November 4, November 22, and November 24, 1938, Yeats papers, Humanities Research Center, University of Texas at Austin. The record of the performance by the Arts Theatre of Cambridge is in the Abbey Theatre Script Room Archives, Abbey Theatre, Dublin.

play May 11–13, 1939. While none of these performances delayed publication of the play, neither, of course, did they expedite the printing of it as Yeats grew increasingly impatient.

In a letter to the Longford printer dated January 10, 1939, Yeats refers to having received galleys, but exactly when he received, corrected, and returned them is not certain.[28] Since he wrote on September 4, 1938, of not yet having received page proofs and would not have expected them before he had corrected galleys, it appears that galleys were corrected sometime before early September. In an undated letter to Higgins he wrote of having received and corrected page proofs, but whether this was written before or after December 24, 1938, is uncertain. On that date he wrote, again to Higgins: "You might let me know if you have received the proofs of 'On the Boiler.' I want *Purgatory* played from 'On the Boiler' version and the text in the hands of the public as soon as possible after the performance. I must of course correct my own proofs."[29]

If the undated letter, which reports that he had read page proofs and explains the problems they presented, was written before December 24, 1938, it is difficult to explain why, in the same letter, Yeats asked Higgins whether he had received proofs, unless the proofs to which he refers are those he already corrected and which he then sent to Higgins to forward to Longford, or, sent directly to Longford with the expectation that the printer would send them to Higgins. In either case, the proofs to which he referred would have been those he had corrected. Since those proofs were already corrected, it is difficult to know what he might have meant when, in the same letter to Higgins, he added: "I must of course correct my own proofs." Alternatively, Yeats might have asked Higgins on December 24 whether he had received proofs because, not yet having received them himself, he wondered whether they had been sent to Higgins. If they had been, he was alerting Higgins to send them on to him so that he, rather than Higgins, could make the corrections. According to this chronology, then, the undated letter would have to have been sent after December 24, 1938. In it he described a new set of problems that arose with the Longford firm, now five months after he had expected the work to be published. Although on December 24, 1938, he had written that he must correct his own proofs, after having corrected them he suggested that Higgins expedite the printing. From the South of France he posted the corrected proofs, along with an explanation and instructions, to Higgins:

> Paged proofs came some days ago and my wife and I have spent a good deal of our time at them. I think we have now corrected everything, but I think it probable that when you look through them you will decide that another revise is necessary. There will be no need for it to be sent here if you would be so kind as to look through it. Indeed much of it is revisions of the press which should be done by somebody who can hear in a day or so by telephone. They have evidently never done printing of our kind before and get into great confusion. Indeed their errors are of a kind that I dont always know how to correct.

[28] Letter to the Longford Printing Press, January 10, 1938, Cliff House, Dalkey.

[29] Letter to F. R. Higgins, December 24, 1938, Yeats papers, Humanities Research Center, University of Texas at Austin.

> They sent no proof of title page and I would be very much obliged if you would arrange about the cover.[30]

On January 10, 1939, Yeats wrote to the Longford printers, explaining some of the difficulties: "I return one set of paged proofs corrected. Please send me a *revise* to the above address, and return to me the *copy with my corrections.* I had a great deal of trouble in making these corrections because you did not return to me the corrected galley proofs when sending paged proof. . . . I shall be glad to receive the revised page proof at your earliest convenience."[31] Although the chronology of the letters might remain uncertain, there can be no doubt that after Yeats corrected galleys he returned them to the Longford printer. The printer prepared page proofs and returned at least two copies of them but failed to return the corrected galleys. Yeats corrected these page proofs without his corrected galleys, kept one *uncorrected* copy, and asked the printer to return to him the *corrected* set when he returned the revise.

There were, then, one set of corrected galleys, which is lost, and two copies of one set of page proofs, both of which were prepared from Yeats's corrected galleys. One copy was sent to Longford and had the author's holograph corrections. It is this set that survives.[32] Yeats could not have seen the second set the printer prepared, which incorporates the revisions he called for on the first page proofs as well as some he called for on the galleys. Therefore the first printing of *On the Boiler* in the Longford edition and the second printing of the Alex.

[30]Letter to F. R. Higgins, n.d., but probably between December 24, 1938, and January 10, 1939. Yeats papers, Humanities Research Center, Austin, Texas. Possibly Richard Finneran is correct in dating the letter in late November, before rather than after Yeats wrote the letter of December 24. See *Editing Yeats's Poems* (New York: St. Martin's Press, 1983). Yeats did write to Edith Shackleton Heald on December 22 that "Higgins owes me four letters" (*Letters,* ed. Wade, p. 910). To Higgins he wrote on November 4: "I forgot to say please worry the Longford people" (Humanities Research Center, University of Texas at Austin). This letter, then, might have been the second in a series of unanswered letters, the third of which was written on November 22 in which Yeats calls for press notices, and the fourth of which would have been the undated letter in which he promises to "write to you [Higgins] about Cuala business etc. in a few days," which he did on December 24 and which letter, the fifth in the series, Higgins presumably answered (letters to F. R. Higgins, Humanities Research Center, University of Texas at Austin). But it is possible that Yeats wrote more than one letter to Higgins before November 4, which would change the chronology of the series, as it is also possible that he wrote more than one letter to Higgins about Cuala business. If the undated letter was written after December 24, and he did write to Higgins as he promised he would in the undated letter, we might expect to find one letter about Cuala business which bears a date later than December 24.

[31]Letter to the Longford Printing Press, January 10, 1938, Cliff House, Dalkey.

[32]Richard Finneran, who mistakenly identified British Library Add. MSS. 55881 and 55892 as "the revised set of proofs with Yeats's further corrections" of *On the Boiler* and *Purgatory,* also mistakenly concludes that the Longford printers "must have complied with Yeats's request." Although there are corrections pertaining chiefly to layout and punctuation, neither those made on the proofs of *On the Boiler* nor those on *Purgatory* are in Yeats's hand. Moreover, on pages 3 and 4 of the proofs of *On the Boiler* are instructions to the printer to correct the text by *Last Poems,* which is probably sufficient evidence that Yeats, who did not see the proofs of *Last Poems,* did not correct those of *On the Boiler* in the British Library. As for the proofs of *Purgatory,* the title page bears the inscription "Corrected by Mrs. Yeats," as indeed the hand appears to be hers. The upper left corner of page 337 of *Purgatory* bears the stamped imprint "THIRD PROOF" and the lower left corner bears the stamped imprint "R. & R. CLARK, Ltd., 12 JUL 1939, EDINBURGH." Also on the lower left foot of the page is printed "VOL. V." The pagination, together with these facts, indicate the proofs, which Yeats could not have seen, were of an edition of his collected work being prepared by Macmillan, but which was never published. See *Editing Yeats's Poems,* p. 115, n. 20.

Thom edition raise certain textual problems that remain to be resolved.[33] But the stages of composition of *Purgatory,* Yeats's decision to append the play to "On the Boiler," and the circumstances surrounding their publication are considerations that provoke fresh readings of the play (and of Yeats's later writings) even as other themes emerge in the light of the manuscript materials: the relation between Yeats and his fictional surrogates, between fathers and sons, pollution and purification, vision and history, and between politics and art, particularly drama and especially tragedy—themes that recurred throughout his career and converged in these texts with extraordinary energy and dramatic efficiency. The essay and the play, both composed and the one performed on the threshold of the outbreak of the Second World War, revived with fresh urgency, as Yeats readily knew they would, the question of his politics.

"On the Boiler" and "Purgatory"

About *On the Boiler* what needs to be kept in mind is that in each section of the essay, the essay as a whole, and the entire publication including *Purgatory,* Yeats advances an argument and then proceeds to devalue or repudiate the view he seemed to uphold. He thus asserts both his convictions and his doubts. Such alternations are especially evident in the first major portion of the essay, "To-morrow's Revolution," which anticipates the skepticism he directs against his own thought in the second part; the essay as a whole prepares for the crystallization of his doubt in *Purgatory.* The tone of the first half of "On the Boiler" is confident, strident, and moralistic; the tone of the second is increasingly reflective, self-effacing, and skeptical.[34] Yeats's argument about the vexed question of eugenic reform, an argument that since the time of antiquity has been about fathers and sons or patriarchal lineage, is evident early in the essay. Throughout, Yeats amplifies an anecdote about his father with which he introduces the essay—an anecdote that tells of his father's violence against him—and by way of which he distinguishes his own from his father's behavior and beliefs. As the essay unfolds, Yeats distinguishes the Irish from the English, most particularly over the issue of "intelligence tests," whose worth he repudiates as a means of objectively measuring who is superior to whom. He ranges swiftly over various subjects, yet returns, as though drawn by an irresistible force, to questions of fathers and sons, the English and the Irish, and to art, and particularly to tragedy. Yet, mediated by his concern with power (and necessarily with politics), the topics interlock and overlap almost imperceptibly from paragraph to paragraph, and from section to section. The elision of topics, however, never conceals Yeats's concern with Ireland.

"On the Boiler" is marked by an acute sense of Irish nationalism, but it needs to be said that Yeats's nationalism issues from the political and cultural antagonism that characterized his own as well as Ireland's relations with England over the years. The attention it commands

[33] Wade, *Bibliography,* p. 201.
[34] For a fuller discussion see my article in *Bulletin of Research in the Humanities,* 21 (1978): 349–368.

in the essay, and, although more obliquely, in *Purgatory*, is equally strong in his earlier writings.

Yeats identified himself with the Irish tradition and from it drew, in addition to much else, confirmation of his view of the vatic role of the poet.[35] The historic fear of English aggrandizement which kindled his nationalism prompted his defense of the Gaelic tongue and the Irish shore. In the middle sections of "On the Boiler" the same political impulse informs his defense of art, particularly drama, and especially tragic drama. He rejects the art of the "commercial" nations, as he had since the 1890s, and again restates without modification his views about tragedy, the afterlife, history, and personality.

> The arts are all the bridal chambers of joy. No tragedy is legitimate unless it leads some great character to his final joy. Polonius may go out wretchedly, but I can hear the dance music in "Absent thee from felicity awhile," or in Hamlet's speech over the dead Ophelia, and what of Cleopatra's last farewells, Lear's rage under the lightning, Oedipus sinking down at the story's end into an earth "riven" by love? Some Frenchman has said that farce is the struggle against a ridiculous object, comedy against a movable object, tragedy against an immovable; and because the will, or energy, is greatest in tragedy, tragedy is the more noble; but I add that "will or energy is eternal delight," and when its limit is reached it may become a pure, aimless joy, though the man, the shade, still mourns his lost object. It has, as it were, thrust up its arms towards those angels who have, as Villiers de L'Isle Adam quotes from St. Thomas Aquinas, returned into themselves in an eternal moment.[36]

With a keen eye for isolating moments of tragic joy in others' plays, Yeats praises scenes and draws attention to moments when defeat yields to triumph, joy transfigures dread. He contrasts his admiration for such moments with his contempt for Flecker's *Hassan* with its "wanton, morbid cruelty" (p. 35). He might well have been thinking of *Hassan* as he drafted versions of *Purgatory*, which even in its final form has been abjured for its violence. Such abjuration Yeats himself might have acknowledged, particularly in the scenario and first verse version. He did revise though, and such revisions were made in response to his admonitions inspired by Flecker's play. Yet, in writing *Purgatory* Yeats did not emulate *Oedipus at Colonus*, as might have been expected. But neither do Sophocles' plays, in contrast to Yeats's version of them, resemble the kind of tragedy Yeats describes. Nothing he wrote about *Purgatory* indicates the scene he would have isolated to exemplify the "eternal delight" or "aimless joy" he required of others' tragedies. Yet, he was not silent about the legend of Oedipus. He mentions *Oedipus the King* and *Oedipus at Colonus* (as well as

[35]See Phillip L. Marcus, *Yeats and the Beginning of the Irish Renaissance* (Ithaca: Cornell University Press, 1970); Jon Stallworthy, *Vision and Revision in Yeats's Last Poems* (London: Oxford University Press, 1969), pp. 1–38; and Peter Ure, *Yeats and Anglo-Irish Literature: Critical Essays*, ed. C. J. Rawson (Liverpool: Liverpool University Press, 1974), pp. 61–81.

[36]*On the Boiler* (Dublin: Cuala, 1939), p. 35.

Sophocles) frequently; he wrote a number of plays, like *Purgatory,* modeled after some episode in the legend, and maintained an interest in perfecting his versions of the Oedipus plays throughout his poetic career.[37] Between 1884 and 1927 he returned to the Oedipus legend on no less than five occasions, but not until he wrote *A Vision* was the importance of the legend and the man clear to him.

Yeats describes the death scene in *Oedipus at Colonus* as though it had actually occurred:

> Oedipus lay upon the earth at the middle point between four sacred objects, was there washed as the dead are washed, and thereupon passed with Theseus to the wood's heart until amidst the sound of thunder earth opened "riven by love," and he sank down soul and body into the earth.[38]

To this fictional Oedipus, he opposes Christ, who, "crucified standing up, went into the abstract sky soul and body." Then, as though Oedipus were historical rather than fictional: "I see him altogether separated from Plato's Athens, from all that talk of the Good and the One, from all that cabinet of perfection, an image from Homer's age."[39] But Yeats's eye is fixed on Oedipus; although it is clear that he has Sophocles' plays in mind, it is equally clear that the plays merely provide an occasion for amplifying his fiction of history:

> When it was already certain that he must bring himself under his own curse did he not still question, and when answered as the Sphinx had been answered, stricken with the horror that is in *Gulliver* and in the *Fleurs du Mal,* did he not tear out his own eyes? He raged against his sons and this rage was noble, not from some general idea, some sense of public law upheld, but because it seems to contain all life, and the daughter who served him as did Cordelia Lear—he too a man of Homer's kind—seemed less attendant upon an old railing rambler than upon genius itself.[40]

Yeats addresses this fictional event—a fusion of Sophocles' imagined world and his own—as though it were historical: "He knew nothing but his mind, and yet because he spoke that mind, fate possessed it and kingdoms changed according to his blessing and his cursing. Delphi, that rock at the earth's navel, spoke through him and though men shuddered and drove him away they spoke of ancient poetry, praising the boughs overhead, the grass under foot, Colonus and its horses."[41] Although Yeats apprehends the situation that captivated

[37]For the central role Oedipus plays in *A Vision* (New York: Macmillan, 1956), see pp. 27–29. Note Yeats's use of the Sophoclean chorus in *On the Boiler*: "I would be praised as a man, / That in my words and my deeds I have kept those laws in mind" (p. 31). Richard Ellmann notes the importance of Oedipus for Yeats: "After first handling the subject in an unpublished play written in 1884, [he] returns to it in 1892 in a poem, 'The Death of Cuchulain,' turns the same story into a play in 1903, makes two translations of *Oedipus Rex,* the first in 1912, the second in 1927, and writes another play involving parricide, *Purgatory,* shortly before his death"; Ellmann, *Yeats: The Man and the Masks* (New York: Dutton, 1948), p. 22. See also Frederic D. Grab, "Yeats's *King Oedipus,*" *Journal of English and Germanic Philology,* 71 (1972): 336–354.

[38]*A Vision,* p. 27.

[39]Ibid., pp. 27 and 28.

[40]Ibid.

[41]Ibid.

Sophocles' imagination—the pariah who is blessed by the gods, is abhorred by men, and yet yields power to the living who bury their bones—neither the psychological moment nor Sophocles' dramatic renderings diverts his attention from Oedipus: "I think that he lacked compassion, seeing that it must be compassion for himself, and yet stood nearer to the poor than saint or apostle, and I mutter to myself stories of Crickmaa, or of the roadside bush withered by Raftery's curse."[42] He moves from Oedipus to the saints, and then to Irish versions of comparable figures. Finally, as he had promised earlier in *A Vision,* he concludes with a suggestion of who the divinity will be.

> What if Christ and Oedipus or, to shift the names, Saint Catherine of Genoa and Michael Angelo, are two scales of a balance, the two butt-ends of a seesaw? What if every two thousand and odd years something happens in the world to make one sacred, the other secular; one wise, the other devilish? What if there is an arithmetic or geometry that can exactly measure the slope of a balance, the dip of a scale, and so date the coming of that something?[43]

Oedipus serves as his model because he "knew nothing but his mind"; knowing nothing but his mind, energy and will drove him to "aimless joy." What made it possible, Yeats had asked, for Oedipus' energy and will to transform his fate and alter the course of history? He derives his answer from his own imagined world rather than from a consideration of the dramatic context Sophoces created for his fictional hero. He addresses the fiction as if it were true and invents a historical Oedipus who is really an imagined prototype of the new divinity he promises to proclaim in *A Vision* and to whom he returned, imaginatively, in the writing of *Purgatory* and "On the Boiler." Once we see that Yeats regards Oedipus as a heroic model for the new cycle of history we are less surprised that in *On the Boiler* he treats *Oedipus the King* and *Oedipus at Colonus* as though they were one rather than two plays, ignores their distinctly different imaginative conceptions, and is inattentive to the lapse of time that separates their composition.

In *A Vision* Yeats brings the last moments of Oedipus' life into sharp focus. In Sophocles' version, the final scene of *Oedipus at Colonus* marks the reversal of the fate of Oedipus from a man cursed for no particular reason that humans can understand to a man who is blessed, again for no particular reason. Yeats, however, accounts for Oedipus' blessing: his "aimless joy" marks the supreme moment of the consummation of his relentless will or energy. At the end of the play Oedipus "knew nothing but his mind; and yet because he spoke that mind fate possessed it and kingdoms changed according to his blessing and his cursing." Will or energy leads to the "aimless joy," to the triumph over intellect which otherwise prevents the release of this consuming moment. Writing to Dorothy Wellesley, Yeats mentions why *On Baile's Strand* (performed with *Purgatory* during the August Abbey Theatre Festival) pleased him. Cuchulain, who, after learning that he has slain his own son, meets his death in madness, fighting the waves, seemed to him "a heroic figure" because, at that moment, "he was creative joy separated from fear."[44] Of *Purgatory* he mentions nothing but the actors. Is

[42] Ibid.
[43] Ibid., pp. 28–29.
[44] *Letters,* ed. Wade, p. 913.

his silence significant or did he fail to see the morbid cruelty of his play? Does he in fact present the Old Man as a modern heir to Oedipus, as one who "knew nothing but his own mind and who changed the fate of history as well as his own"? One need not speculate. The final scene of *Purgatory*, when the Old Man's lust subsides as he offers a prayer, contrasts sharply with Yeats's reading of the end of *Oedipus at Colonus*.

If Yeats had understood Oedipus as a literary hero and patterned his own creation accordingly, the Old Man in *Purgatory* might have been capable of representing aimless joy, as Cuchulain is in *On Baile's Strand*. Although Yeats seems to recognize in Cuchulain "creative joy separated from fear," he seems as inattentive to the dramatic context of the action of his own play as he is to that of Sophocles': *On Baile's Strand*, with its double plot of blind and dumb men stealing bread while Cuchulain fights the waves, anticipates the derision Yeats casts upon his own poetic quest, particularly in *The Herne's Egg* and other late plays. But it anticipates other problems as well: the one set aesthetic and intellectual, which presented itself to him as long as he remained persuaded of the central importance for his art of rendering moments of tragic joy dramatically; the other of dramatizing heroism in a world thought to be exclusively historical. The successive revisions of the verse drafts of *Purgatory* illumine the final version, which, without the manuscripts, could not as plausibly be read as Yeats's boldest and most vigorous effort to dramatize (rather than try to resolve) the insoluble problems to which his own vision had brought him. By reducing the Old Man's knowledge of himself yet preserving his grotesque behavior, and by deleting from the play any persuasive notion that the mother can save herself (or be saved by anyone else), he merged irony of character and irony of situation. Finally, in spite of the Old Man's wish to make a difference to the suffering he and his mother share, the final version of the play dramatizes the decidedly inclusive irony of history itself. The Old Man's prayer at the end of the play,

> O God,
> Release my mother's soul from its dream!
> Mankind can do no more. Appease
> The misery of the living and the remorse of the dead. [TS7, ll. 219–222]

cannot be spoken joyfully nor can the Old Man be thought to represent joy separated from fear; although the Old Man is sufficiently reflective to be aware of his failure, in his revisions Yeats carefully and deliberately excised the Old Man's knowledge of himself and therefore of his own share in having caused that failure.

The Old Man's impotent prayer at the end of *Purgatory* is strikingly similar to Yeats's response to his own reading of history. On the one hand, the Old Man recognizes that his mother is locked into her past as Yeats believed historical events were determined by antecedent events. On the other hand, the Old Man anticipates releasing his mother's dream from its past, as Yeats himself fashions a version of history that would release him, imaginatively, from the recurrent cycles of change. *Purgatory* cannot be said to contain any joyful moments resembling those Yeats praises in others' plays in the last sections of "On the Boiler." Although the play violates his own prescriptions for tragedy, it serves, nevertheless, as the appropriate epilogue to the essay. Had Yeats lived, it is unlikely he would have turned his attention to so lurid a violation. He was not in the habit of asking himself whether his discursive, poetic, and dramatic writings confirmed one another. He was, however, keenly aware of the adverse relation between beliefs and action, particularly action or conflict in the form of argument. For Yeats, argument, whether political or poetic, was a mode of discovery. It was a means for performing what he called the ''play of the mind.''[45] In allowing the mind to play, one discovered, as Yeats thought Shakespeare had, that ''he was an altogether different man to what he thought himself, and held altogether different beliefs.''[46] Political or poetic argument that failed to yield discovery produced hearts of stone.

Yeats's enactment of the argument of ''On the Boiler''—recurrently unsettling his convictions, persistently asserting his confidence and his doubts, deliberately balancing truths with countertruths—is as powerful a figure for the argument as for the theme, as Yeats called it, of the essay itself. The meaning of the argument lies in the significance of the dramatic enactment as well as its theme. Finally, argument and theme are inseparable.

In the opening passages of ''On the Boiler,'' Yeats identifies himself with mad McCoy; toward the conclusion of the essay, after the sections on tragic drama, he returns to the mad ship's carpenter once again: ''The old man on the boiler has been silent about religion, but soon this occasional publication, probably in its next number, will print his words upon that subject without tact or discretion.''[47] Irony is more characteristic of Yeats than tact. In the last section of ''On the Boiler'' he writes: ''Of late I have tried to understand in its practical details the falsehood that is in all knowledge, science more false than philosophy, but that too false. Yet, unless we cling to knowledge, until we have examined its main joints, it comes at us with staring eyes.''[48] His irony serves less to protect than to release him to confess to historical eddies of thought, feeling, and perception in and out of literature.

In the final sections of ''On the Boiler,'' Yeats is doubtful of the beliefs he formulates even in this essay. And yet, the final sections, although more boldly articulated, do not stand outside of the argument. They are as essential a part as the paragraphs about his father and John Stuart Mill, intelligence tests, eugenic reform, science and myth, unity of being, tragedy, and Oedipus. As though his swift reversals of thought and feeling gather a momentum of their own, he marvels at the energy of his own mind in its refusal to rest in the ease of satisfaction. He seems at moments to know ''nothing but his mind.'' *Purgatory* is not the dramatic animation of the beliefs expressed in ''On the Boiler'' any more than the essay is a simple pronouncement. The Old Man of *Purgatory,* like Yeats, is vituperative; unlike Yeats, he is wholly ignorant of himself. In the process of revising the character of the Old Man, shaping a figure whose self-deception deepens rather than yields to self-knowledge, Yeats himself was aware of the quarrel from which his arguments drew their imaginative life. Thus in the final version of *Purgatory* the prayer at the end is a response to the history of his own creation. In ''On the Boiler'' Yeats views history as a destructive force, but the only force. If

[45]*Autobiography,* p. 218.

[46]Letter, April 20, 1929, quoted by Richard Ellmann, *The Identity of Yeats* (New York: Oxford University Press, 1954), p. 42.

[47]*On the Boiler,* p. 32.

[48]Ibid., p. 36.

we were confident, as he is not, that science were true, eugenics could save us. Yeats was as skeptical of such facile solutions as he was of the efficacy of the Old Man's prayer, which marks an ironic defeat that heralds a new Oedipus. The Old Man is neither the hero *A Vision* proclaims nor the spokesman for Yeats's ''beliefs'' but the parodic double of Yeats's own thought.

Transcription Principles and Procedures

Every page of transcription is accompanied by a photo-facsimile. Readers who wish to *see* what Yeats wrote can easily compare the original document with my transcription. There are bound to be differences of opinion over what Yeats actually wrote: his hand, never easy to read, is especially difficult in these manuscripts. Approximately one fourth of the scenario is written in pencil, which has either faded or was never very dark; the first full version of the play contains pages that are crowded with revisions whose cancellation lines often obscure earlier versions of portions of the play. Moreover, Yeats composed rapidly, as though buoyed by a rush of creative energy: often a single stroke of the pen designates three or four letters; often words begun seem to fade as the pen moves swiftly to form new words. Particularly in early versions of *Purgatory,* he was inattentive to punctuation, to the use of lower and upper case letters, and he was even inattentive to syntax. Occasionally, he simply omitted words, although the meaning of a line requires that the word be there as, for example: ''& he has been a public house for a drink'' ($P4^r$69). In solving these and other problems such as spelling, illegible words, the use of carets, I have been guided by the following principles and adopted the conventions that are described below:

1. Often letters appear to be missing or conflated: where there is no reasonable doubt what word Yeats intended, I have transcribed that word in full without comment. For example, the third word on $P1^r$ 7 is transcribed as ''attention'' although the last three letters are indistinct. There are occasional instances where words are misspelled. These have been preserved, even if incorrect. For example, I have not deleted an extra ''d'' from the word ''shaddow'' as it appears on $P1^r$ 13 and I have not deleted an extra ''b'' from the word ''ribbs'' as it appears on VAJ^r. In both of these instances the same word appears within a few lines spelled in the conventional way and in each instance the misspelling appears to be caused by haste and inattentiveness to such matters. Similarly, I have not corrected the spelling of such words as ''pigstie,'' ''rumagged,'' and ''hoffs'' as they occasionally appear in the manuscripts. In other instances I have preserved Yeats's spelling, although it is inaccurate or, as in an instance of $VA3^r$ 8, the word ''there'' ought to read ''they're'' or, perhaps, ''they are.'' Since ''there'' is distinct, and allows for a degree of suggestive ambiguity Yeats might have wanted to preserve, it seemed preferable to transcribe the word as it appears. In this instance and in others like it I have called attention to the problem in notes keyed to the line. Where Yeats inadvertently omitted punctuation, as in $P8^r$ 141–142, I have preferred to allow readers to supply the punctuation called for by the sense of the line.

2. Words that are sometimes broken by a space are joined, as on VA1^{r} 11 where "game keeper" is transcribed as "gamekeeper." Similarly, on VA9K^{r} 7 "no body" is transcribed as "nobody." Where spaces are greater than those Yeats normally left between letters of one word, the space has been preserved.
3. Symbols for illegible words and editorial conjectures:

[?]	a totally unintelligible word
stran [?]	a partially unintelligible word
[? ? ?]	several totally unintelligible words
[~~?~~]	a cancelled and totally unintelligible word
[?and]	a conjectural reading (used only when the editor feels more than ordinary uncertainty)
[/by/?of]	equally possible conjectural readings

4. Overwritings are indicated thus: {R
remorse = "remorse" converted to "Remorse."
5. There are throughout the drafts certain obscure marks or blots, which may have been made accidentally. In cases where their significance has not been determined, they are silently omitted.
6. Cancellation of single lines or of words within a line is indicated by horizontal cancellation lines. (These lines are straight even where Yeats's were wavy.) Where Yeats intended to cancel an entire word but only struck through part of it, the cancellation line in the transcription extends through the entire word. However, even when it seems likely that Yeats meant to cancel an entire phrase or line, no word that he did not at least partially cancel is cancelled in the transcriptions.
7. Cancellation of entire passages is indicated by vertical brackets in the left margin. (See item 12, below.) Arrows indicating relocation of words and passages also only approximate the originals. Where typographical limitations make it impossible to print a marginal revision in its actual position, it is given immediately below the transcription of the page on which it occurs. Arrows leading from such passages are not reproduced.
8. Yeats's "stet" marks are preserved, as are his underscorings to indicate italics. All other instructional inscriptions such as "P. T. O." and "see back" have been recorded. Caret symbols that Yeats placed just below the line are raised to line level.
9. In the transcriptions of typescript material, minor and obvious typing errors are recorded only when they are significant, but all holograph corrections of typescript are indicated.
10. Problems in the transcriptions of words and passages are discussed in footnotes keyed to line numbers in the margin of the transcriptions.
11. Although spacing and relative positions of words and lines generally approximate the originals, a degree of typographical regularization is employed in regard to such elements as indentations and the placement of above-the-line revisions.
12. The following typographical conventions have been used to represent various physical features of the texts:

roman	blue-black ink (variations of ink color are indicated in notes)
italic	pencil
~~cancellation line~~	deletion
boldface	typescript

Purgatory

MANUSCRIPTS, WITH TRANSCRIPTIONS AND PHOTOGRAPHIC REPRODUCTIONS

With the exception of one leaf, the manuscript versions of *Purgatory* were written on white wove loose-leaf paper, punched with three holes and having pale blue-green horizontal bars 6/10 cm wide, and a double red top margin rule. The paper measures 22.9 cm × 18.0 cm and is watermarked WALKERS / Loose Leaf / MADE IN GT BRITAIN. Yeats used similar paper for *The Death of Cuchulain* and several of the *Last Poems*. He kept leaves in a ring binder, where they could be rearranged during the process of composition.

The Scenario, in folder 1 of NLI MS 8771, consists of eight pages, each of which bears a number on the upper right margin of the recto. Yeats composed in prose, leaving all versos blank except page 1, on which he began to sketch a few lines of dialogue, and page 8, which bears directional lines that connect with a page that has not survived. He composed in dark blue-black ink, pencil, and blue ink.

The earliest extant verse draft of the play is in folder 2 of NLI MS 8771, and consists of twelve leaves, each of which is paginated, although pages 7^{v} and 9^{v} bear unrecognizable symbols in the upper right margin. Pages 4, 6, and 8 appear to be missing. All of the leaves are in blue-black ink except for two that represent intermediary stages of composition and are in black ink.

The second and final manuscript version of the play is in folder 3 of NLI MS 8771, and consists of twelve leaves, all numbered in sequence and all of which are written in blue-black ink except for the verso of leaf 8, which contains the ballad "O Glory," by F. R. Higgins. Yeats probably imagined the poem might find a place in *Purgatory,* but decided against it. It is written in blue-green ink and with a nib heavier than the one used elsewhere in the draft.

One leaf belonging to the manuscripts of *Purgatory* is in folder 36 of NLI MS 13,593 and represents an intermediary stage of composition between the writing of the scenario and the first draft version of the play. Although the leaf bears the letter "B" in the upper left margin of the verso, this one, and another that contains a sketch of the stage set for *Purgatory* and bears the letter "D," also in the upper left margin, and also in folder 36 of NLI MS 13,593, do not appear to be part of a more extensive sequence of leaves. The letters were probably inserted either by Curtis Bradford or by some other scholar who identified odd leaves with letters such as those that appear on *The Death of Cuchulain* manuscripts. The leaf marked "D" is in the folder 36 of NLI MS 13,593 and is written on paper that measures the same and bears the same watermark as the leaf marked "B," also written in blue-black ink. The sketch corresponds so closely to the scene envisioned in the scenario, and departs so greatly from stage directions that appear in later versions of the play, it is likely that it was drawn before he began the verse draft.

One leaf of manuscript belonging to *Purgatory* is among the Yeats papers in the possession of Senator Michael B. Yeats, Cliff House, Dalkey. It represents a stage of revision intermediary between the first version of lines g and lines h–k, TS 5^{r}, the stage directions that precede them, and the final version on TS5 6^{v}. The leaf therefore belongs with TS5 and is discussed more fully with the materials contained in NLI MS 8771#5.

For the purposes of analysis, the transcriptions that follow are separated into three groups:

Manuscripts of the Scenario
Manuscripts of the first version of *Purgatory*
Manuscripts of the second version of *Purgatory*

To facilitate identification I have assigned a letter and number to every leaf of manuscript material. I have preserved as far as possible Yeats's own numbering. A "P" before the number indicates that the leaf was part of the prose draft; "P" followed by a number and the letter "i" indicates that the leaf was intermediary between the prose scenario and first draft; the leaf marked "S1^{r}" indicates that it represents Yeats's sketch for the stage set. "VA" followed by a number indicates that the leaf was part of the first verse version of the play; "VB" followed by a number indicates that the leaf was part of the second verse version of the play. "VB" followed by a number and the letter "i" indicates that the leaf was part of an intermediary stage between two leaves of MS 8771#3. Superscript ^{r} and ^{v} indicate recto and verso of a leaf as used by Yeats. All but one of the leaves are in the National Library of Ireland, where they are arranged by folder number. One leaf is in the private collection of Senator Michael B. Yeats. The location of each leaf is given in the list that follows:

P1^{r} NLI 8771(1)
P1^{v} NLI 8771(1)
P2^{r} NLI 8771(1)
P3^{r} NLI 8771(1)
P4^{r} NLI 8771(1)
P5^{r} NLI 8771(1)
P6^{r} NLI 8771(1)
P7^{r} NLI 8771(1)
P8^{r} NLI 8771(1)
P2i^{v} NLI 13,593(36)
S1^{v} NLI 13,593(36)
P8i^{v} NLI 8771(1)
VA1^{r} NLI 8771(2)
VA1^{v} NLI 8771(2)
VA2^{r} NLI 8771(2)
VA2^{v} NLI 8771(2)
VA3^{r} NLI 8771(2)
VA5^{r} NLI 8771(2)
VA7^{r} NLI 8771(2)
VA7^{v} NLI 8771(2)
VA9^{r} NLI 8771(2)
VA9^{v} NLI 8771(2)

VA10^{r}	NLI 8771(2)
VA10^{v}	NLI 8771(2)
VA11^{r}	NLI 8771(2)
VA11^{v}	NLI 8771(2)
VA12^{r}	NLI 8771(2)
VA13^{r}	NLI 8771(2)
VA13^{v}	NLI 8771(2)
VA13i^{r}	NLI 8771(2)
VA14^{r}	NLI 8771(2)
VB1^{r}	NLI 8771(3)
VB2^{r}	NLI 8771(3)
VB2^{v}	NLI 8771(3)
VB3^{r}	NLI 8771(3)
VB3^{v}	NLI 8771(3)
VB4^{r}	NLI 8771(3)
VB4^{v}	NLI 8771(3)
VB5^{r}	NLI 8771(3)
VB5^{v}	NLI 8771(3)
VB6^{r}	NLI 8771(3)
VB7^{r}	NLI 8771(3)
VB7^{v}	NLI 8771(3)
VB8^{r}	NLI 8771(3)
VB8^{v}	NLI 8771(3)
VB9^{r}	NLI 8771(3)
VB9^{v}	NLI 8771(3)
VB10a^{r}	NLI 8771(3)
VB10a^{v}	NLI 8771(3)
VB11^{r}	NLI 8771(3)
VB11^{v}	NLI 8771(3)
VB11^{v}	NLI 8771(3)
VB11i^{r}	NLI 8771(3)
VB12^{r}	NLI 8771(3)

Each line of the scenario has been assigned a number to which the notes are keyed, and each line of every page of the first and second verse drafts has been assigned a number beginning anew on each page. The bracketed line numbers given for each page indicate the lines of Yeats's final text to which the text on that page corresponds.

Manuscripts of the Scenario

The scenario consists of eight leaves. On the verso of leaf P1 Yeats sketched four lines of dialogue, added revisions of two lines that appear on leaf P2^r, and three lines of prose. Otherwise, all of the versos are blank, except for page P8i^v, which contains three lines written in blue rather than blue-black ink and bears two directional lines neither one of which connects with pages VA1^r (or any other pages of folders 2 or 3) or with any other leaves currently known to exist. The first half of line a of leaf P8i^v—"Answer me that?"—appears in folder 2, page VA1^v, but the second half—"Study that house"—appears in folder 3, page VB1^r, but the first half does not appear. Yeats incorporated the revisions of lines a–b on page P8i^v into the first verse version, pages VA1^v and VA2^v, revised them further on page VB2^v, and eventually incorporated them into the earliest typescript, which is catalogued in the National Library of Ireland as MS 8771#6. Line c of page P8i^v—"Its like—no matter what its like"—appears on page VB1^r of the second verse version. Therefore, although it is inscribed on the verso of the last page of the scenario, it seems likely that page P8i^v represents an intermediary stage of revision between the first and second verse drafts. All of the other pages are written in blue-black ink, except for the lines beginning with the second to the last on P2^r and continuing for the following 31 lines, which are in pencil. Lines 69 to the end are written in the same shade of blue-black ink with what appears to be the same nib. Whether Yeats composed in one or more sittings is impossible to know. (Although Curtis Bradford is right in his observation that "the backs of pages one and eight have been used for revision," page P8i^v was not a revision of the scenario as he assumes it to be.)[1]

There is something to be gained from noticing those aspects of the scenario Yeats chose to emphasize, and those he preferred to subdue or delete entirely, as he evolved the first, and then second, versions of the play. Bradford remarks that: "After he [Yeats] had recorded this dreadful vision in the scenario, Yeats had still to clothe the bare bones of his plot with the flesh of detail, and he had to put the whole into verse."[2] Bradford would not have needed to qualify his conclusion if he had been able to transcribe the scenario more fully. He would have been obliged, however, to comment on Yeats's successive revisions of the scene of the Old Man's murder of his father and of his changing conception of himself.

In his revision of the scenario, as he moved from prose to verse, Yeats retained the

[1]Curtis B. Bradford, *Yeats at Work* (Carbondale: Southern Illinois University Press, 1965), p. 295.
[2]Ibid., p. 297.

sequence of dialogue and action as he had sketched them in the scenario. The six lines of dialogue and three lines of prose on page P1^{v} represent a stage of revision which probably followed after Yeats completed the writing of the scenario. Yeats introduced the word "transgressions" here for the first time, and although it appears nowhere else in the scenario the word is central to the conception of later versions of the play. Page P8^{r}, lines 132–142, contains the essential passage that Yeats needed to clarify: what difference can the living make to the suffering of the dead? How much knowledge, if any, of the "evil" consequences of their actions do shades have? Can purification be accomplished by the living without polluting further what one seeks to purify?

Two other leaves belonging to *Purgatory* are in the National Library of Ireland and are catalogued as MS 13,593(36). Page P2i^{v} contains twenty-two lines of prose dialogue which are revisions of page P1^{r} of the scenario and, in turn, anticipate further revisions on page VA2^{r} of MS 8771#2. Yeats's script, which is typically difficult to decipher, is, perhaps, no more difficult here, although far more words have been omitted than are omitted on other leaves. He ignored syntax and punctuation more than he typically did in early stages of composition. He composed as though consumed by an urgency to get onto paper what might otherwise be lost.

It is likely that Yeats composed page P2i^{v} sometime after he began the scenario and either just before or after he completed it. His having composed it on the verso of "Long-legged Fly," which he completed in April, suggests that he composed some or all of the scenario, set it aside briefly to work on the poem, and, while returning to "Long-legged Fly" or other poems, he somewhat hastily sketched the lines for *Purgatory* which appear on the verso page in folder 36. Ordinarily, he reserved for revision the versos of manuscripts on which he was working as indeed he did the versos of MSS 8771#2 and #3. There are very few leaves of *Purgatory* revised on versos left blank for revision; the revisions on page P2i^{v} are of interest chiefly because they represent Yeats's exploration of precisely the problem of how the Old Man views himself—a problem that required considerable adjustment before Yeats arrived at the conception of the play which satisfied both his dramatic impulse and the vision of the world he finally dramatized.

In the scenario the house is in shadow, one stream of moonlight falls on a blasted tree, while another falls on front stage on the Old Man and the Boy. This much is the same in the revision on page P1i^{v}. Yeats revised exactly what the Old Man and the Boy identify as being evil. In the scenario the dialogue between the Old Man and the Boy is over whether the house—Yeats cancelled the word "house" and added "place"—is horrible, or whether it seems horrible because it is in the shadow cast by the hill. The Old Man says it is dark, evil, and horrible, whereas the Boys says it merely seems that way because of the shadow: it is "no worse than any other place." Finally, the Old Man blames the horrible house for the fact that he and the Boy must live by peddling needles and spools. It is only later in the scenario—much later, after Yeats began to compose in pencil, and after the Old Man narrates the fall of the house and the murder of his father—that he refers to himself as evil. Indeed, it is only after the narrative in which the Old Man establishes the link between himself and the evil of the house that Yeats introduces the dynastic theme. Sons inherit the sins of their fathers. It is also worth noting that in the scenario, as I have pointed out in the introduction, the narrative description is more lurid than in subsequent versions even as the account itself is more lurid. In the scenario, although nowhere else in the manuscripts, the Old Man strangles his father and, after having killed him, leaves him in the house to be consumed by the flames. It is as though the Old Man, after having described the patricide, identifies himself as evil—but only then. The scenario does not begin with the Old Man's identification of himself as evil: it is the house that is evil. The brief sketch on page P1i^{v} marks the beginning of the revision to which Yeats subjected the figures of the Boy and the Old Man.

Rather than being calm, unafraid, and reassuring, the Boy is distraught, fearful, and menaced by every object. Furthermore, whereas in the scenario the Old Man found the place evil, in the revised versions he, not the Boy, remarks that the place is no worse than any other, that the shadow of the hill makes it seem dreadful. The dialogue is essentially the same. But the characters seem to have exchanged lines. There are, however, some additions. The boy reiterates his fear: he hates the tree, he hates the house. The Old Man explains it is not the house but those living in it and those who live there still, who are evil. The illegibility of the script combined with the broken syntax makes it difficult to know whether the Old Man's reference to "two evil brutes" is to those who live in the house—shades of his mother and father—or to himself and the Boy. But either way one decides to read that line, the Old Man is locating evil either in himself and his son, or in his mother and father. Perhaps the ambiguity of the broken syntax reflects Yeats's own indecision. Eventually, as he conceived the final version, both are "evil." In addition to these revisions, Yeats introduced into the Old Man's lines the image of the moonlit tree as a figure for a purified soul that has passed from purgatory. Probably at the same time, he turned his attention to matters of stagecraft and sketched the stage set on the verso of the second leaf belonging to *Purgatory* in MS 13,895(36), which is identified here as page S1^{r}.

Page S1^{r} corresponds so closely to the scene envisioned in the scenario, page P1^{r}, lines 1–5, that it is likely that it was drawn either before or after Yeats composed the scenario, perhaps during the writing of it, and most likely at the same time as he composed on P1i^{v} his revision of pages P1^{r} and P2^{r}. MS 8771#2 does not contain stage directions, nor does MS 8771#3. Page VB1^{r}, however, calls for "a ruined house & a bare tree in the background. Moonlight," but nothing more. These directions are elaborated more fully in MS 8771#6, page 1^{r}, which suggests that if the sketch had been drawn after the writing of the scenario, the tree would certainly have been placed in a different position. The position it occupies in the sketch corresponds to the one described in the scenario and those passages he revised which appear on page P1i^{v}.

1

Scenario

A bare ruined house. A large window, a door. The house is in
shadow [illegible] one side, & above a grey cloud is half—
a [illegible] black tree shows white in moon light. A [illegible]
a moon [illegible] falls on the front of stage so that the
characters are well light. Old man & boy carry a
pack: Old man says [illegible]
& [illegible]
house in [illegible]." A dark [illegible] [illegible]. The
boy says it is no worse than any other. [illegible]
of [illegible] The old man
says that where they are is well enough but the
house is dark & horrible. The boy says that
is because the shadow of the hill falls upon it
The old man the boy does not know what he
talking about. That house is horrible. It is because
of that house that he & the boy must live by the
[illegible], [illegible], & [illegible] & shreds of [illegible] & [illegible]
[illegible]. No new [illegible] in that house. The

Scenario 1

1 A ~~hous~~ ruined house. A large window & a door. The house is in
2 shadow. at one side of house above a garden wall or hedge—
3 a ~~tree~~ blasted tree shows white in moon light. A ~~st~~ stream
light
4 of moon ~~li~~ ∧ falls on the front of stage so that the
~~Larg~~ a broken garden seat.
5 characters are well lighted. Old Man & boy carry a
6 pack : Old Man says ~~boy may put down pack~~
7 & ~~pay attention to the place where he is, & it is~~ a
It is place
8 ~~house in front of him~~. A dark evil ~~house~~. The
place
9 boy says it is no worse than any other. ~~The shadow~~
10 of ~~the hill falls upon it. The Old Man The~~ The Old Man
11 says that where they are is well enough but the
12 house is dark & horrible. The boy says that
13 is because the shaddow of the hill falls upon it
14 The Old Man the boy does not know what hes
15 talking about. That house is horrible. It is because
16 of that house that & he the boy must live by ~~pe~~
17 peddling needles, & pins & spools of thread & he has
18 read books. He read them in that house. The

---

12 "it" probably omitted after "that."
13 period probably omitted after "it."
14 "says" probably omitted after "Man."
16 "& he" are written in reverse order.

Boy: You are trying to [illegible] me. [illegible] [illegible] left than in
what you should [illegible] me [illegible] left [illegible] me.

O M, My mother your grandmother lived in the
house, my ~~mother~~ [illegible] ~~was a~~ [illegible] of b
Boy. ~~where is she I [illegible] me~~. They are dead
she is dead & she is here
O M. ~~She is — Ten years ago I saw her~~

The dead ~~return to the places where~~ they play
in purgatory return to the places where they played
to the places of their happiness — they return again & again

a Boy: You are trying to terrify me. Now you [?~~tefts~~] ter me
b with your stick & now you ~~tef~~ terrify me.
c OM. My mother your grand mother lived in that
d house.
~~my mother was a high~~ up la
e Boy. ~~What is that to do with me. They are~~ dead
She is dead & she is there
f OM. ~~She is— Ten years ago I came~~ here
g The dead ~~return to the places where~~ they play
h in purgatory return to the places where they plaid
i to the places of their transgressions—they return again & again

---

Page P1iv was probably composed after Yeats completed the scenario and had begun to revise. It is likely that he abandoned ll. a–b, but they lingered until he composed MS 8771#3 where they reappear in considerably revised form. Lines c–f are revisions of P2r, ll. 33–35. Lines g–i introduce the word "transgressions"; they are later revisions of P2r, ll. 21–24.

boy asks if this is the house he brought him to 2
see. The old ~~man tells him to talk~~ of the
[illegible] ~~[illegible]~~ he says that the dead
return to the places where they lived, & live again over
& over ~~[illegible]~~ the moment when their life
came to a crisis. We come back to this house also
but the two ghosts a man ^or woman^ have come back here to
live there in this house. The boy says that the old
man is as the [illegible] of [illegible]. All he knows is all
lies. when he is not lazy, [illegible] he is lazy told lies.
The old man, So this is that night [illegible] ^[illegible]^ your [illegible]
~~[illegible] [illegible] [illegible] [illegible] [illegible]~~ [illegible]
the [illegible] ~~[illegible] [illegible] [illegible] [illegible]~~ [illegible]
~~[illegible]~~ when one of those two come for the [illegible]
to this house. The boy ^my grandmother [illegible] [illegible] of [illegible]^ ~~[illegible] [illegible] [illegible] [illegible]~~
~~[illegible]~~ grandmother [illegible], she [illegible] was a [illegible] of
Cady. The old man tells him to [illegible] of the
[illegible] and [illegible] as if it were the loveliest thing you
would hear in this world. For a moment you will
hear the [illegible] of horses — for this is when

19 boy asks if that is the house he brought him to

2

20 see. The Old ~~Man tells him to take off~~ the
21 ~~pack & sit down & listen. He~~ says that the dead
22 return to the places where they lived, & live again over
23 & over ~~the evil things [?]~~ the moments when their life
24 came to a crisis. We come back to this hous alive
& a woman
25 but ~~a~~ two ghosts a man∧have come back too they
26 are there in this house. The boy says that the old
27 man is at his lies again. And he knows its all
28 lies. When he is not being beaten he is being told lies.
sixty three
29 The Old Man. So that on that night ~~sixty years~~∧years before
30 ~~at a full moon~~ ~~something happened to~~ ~~two living people~~ & on
31 the ~~anniversary that~~ is ~~the full moon~~ ~~lig~~ ~~now two people~~
32 ~~that died~~ ~~those~~ one of those two came from the fire
my grandmother was a high up lady
33 to this house. The boy ~~You that was grandfathers~~
34 ~~hou~~ grandmothers house, she that was a high up
35 lady. The Old Man tells him to take off the
36 pack ~~as~~ and listen as if it were the last thing you
37 would hear in this world. *In a moment you will*
38 *hear it the hooves of horses—for this is what*

---

20 "Man" probably cancelled by mistake; probably intended to cancel "the."

29 Yeats abandoned the narrative here and allows the Old Man to speak for himself. Hereafter, the narrative is mixed direct and indirect discourse.

31 Probably intended to cancel "is."

33 "says" or a colon omitted after "boy."

3

I saw it ten years ago — all [illegible] burnt [illegible]
of course it was [illegible] years. ~~The boy~~
~~Says there is [illegible] that~~ the house is [illegible] [illegible]
~~The other says~~ this boy's mother was born in
this house from her ancestors — her father was dead
& her mother was an old woman & there
was no one to control her. She married her father's
or her grandfather's groom whom she [illegible] or [illegible]
[illegible], when she had a horse in training. He
was a groom [illegible]. ~~[illegible]~~ [illegible] her
she took a fancy to him. ~~Her friends~~ told them
& he used to go riding with her, & he made love
to her. He followed her — ~~[illegible]~~ she
~~Her own people~~ her own people, ~~her servants~~ tried
tried to stop her but the world [illegible] [illegible]
any — they say she loved her master [illegible]
but they [illegible] [illegible]. ~~She married him~~
~~The boy says [illegible]~~
He married her in the village chapel.

3

39 *I heard ten years ago—all ways at twelve & it*
40 *it comes on this one night of year. ~~The boy~~*
41 *~~says that he does not what the OldM is talking~~ about.*
42 *~~The other says~~ that his mother had inherited*
43 *this house from her ancestors—Her father ~~was~~ dead*
44 *& her mother was an old woman & there*
45 *was no one to control her. He [?met] [?his] father*
46 *the boy grandfather some where on the other side*
in training
47 *of Ireland, where she had a horse ~~running~~ He*
a groom
48 *was a ~~jockey.~~ ~~He followed her back~~ here*
49 *~~Sh took a fancy to him. Her friends~~ told this*
50 *& he used to go riding with her, & he made love*
51 *to. He followed her— ~~every body tried to~~ st*
52 *~~Her own people~~ her own people, ~~her servants~~ even*
53 *tried to stop her but she would not listen to*
54 *any—they say she heard her mother out*
55 *but may be they lied. She ~~married~~ him*
56 *~~in~~ ~~The boy says hed marry her~~*
57 *He married her in the village church.*

---

40 "the" probably omitted before "year."
41 "know" probably omitted before "what"; probably intended to cancel "about."
43 "dead" probably intended as "died."
45 Probably intended "She" not "He."
46 Probably intended "boy's."
48 Probably intended to cancel "here."
51 "her" probably omitted after "to."
54 "any" probably intended as "anyone."

4

The boy says that his father was a groom
Man & [illegible] a rich woman — [illegible]
The old man says he was only a drunken [illegible]
and spent all the money. The young boy says if I married
a rich woman I would have a great time
spending her money. (Sound of a horse
hoofs) ~~The~~ The old man says there is
no — there is no. ~~The boy says he can~~
hear ~~[illegible]~~
cant hear. There is the sound of the horse.
~~He~~ This is their marriage night & he
& he has been to public house for a drink. #
a there she is there now in the window — there
looking. And a the boy at the [illegible]
mother boy of [illegible] months — at the ghost
The boy says: there is no one there. Then

4

58 *The boy says that the father was a great*
59 *man & cajoled a rich woman— ~~And~~*
60 *the Old Man says 'he was [?boy] a drunken scoundrel*
61 *and spent all she had' The [~~?yo~~] boy if I married*
62 *a rich woman I would have a grand time*
63 *spending her money. (sound of a horses*
64 *hoofs) ~~The~~ The Old Man says there it*
65 *is—there it is— ~~Th boy says he~~ can*
66 *~~here may be you can hear it may be~~ you*
67 *cant here. That is the sound of his horse.*
68 *~~He~~ This is their marriage night & he*
69 & he has been a public house for a drink. ~~Th~~
70 A there she is there there in the window—there
71 listening. Look at her boy at your grand
72 mother boy at my mother—at her ghost
73 The boy says that he is mad again—Theres

---

60 Single quotes are used here for the first time.
61 Single quotes or the word "says" omitted before "if."
65 "can" probably intended as "can't."
66 "here" probably intended as "hear"; either "the Old Man says" or single quotes probably omitted before "may be."
67 "here" probably intended as "hear."
69 "& he" in l. 68 are the last words written in pencil; Yeats resumed in ink with these words and neglected to cancel one pair of them; "to" probably omitted before "a."
70 "A" probably intended as "And."

~~You are going mad as your father [illegible]~~ You are beginning [illegible] 8
[illegible], I see the [illegible]
nothing there.) The woman leave the window
then [illegible] the old man shows fight. The old man
says the horse has been stolen. He has rushed
now to the latch & is pulling the horse in
He is half drunk, he is always half drunk
the stable. She has given / let them [illegible]
[illegible] [illegible] [illegible] [illegible] [illegible]
[illegible] [illegible] she [illegible] [illegible] [illegible]
He can [illegible] [illegible] [illegible] [illegible] [illegible] [illegible] [illegible]
[illegible] [illegible] [illegible] [illegible] [illegible] [illegible] [illegible]
~~[illegible] [illegible] [illegible] you are~~ [illegible]. ~~[illegible] [illegible] [illegible] [illegible] the~~
door. He has taken her in their arms. They are
going in - going the marriage bed. ~~[illegible]~~ [illegible]
night - [illegible] night - may be that night I
shall be gotten. That night the night.
If then you are about to beget me - I that
am the most evil [illegible], this boy the 5
most evil [illegible] - ~~this boy that begot~~ is
This is a dark [illegible], a curse that has been
[illegible] in [illegible], to begin. & curse me after the
woman. 7½ He hits the boy - ~~& pulls him to the~~
[illegible] [illegible] [illegible] [illegible] the [illegible] [illegible] the
old man says [illegible] [illegible] [illegible] [illegible] [illegible]. He sees
[illegible] [illegible] [illegible] - [illegible] [illegible] [illegible] [illegible]
whole [illegible] [illegible]

~~You are going mad again pret seeing what does~~ You are lying again \5
pretending to see what does not exist
74 Nothing there. The woman leaves the window
75 blind which ~~re~~ slowly fades. The Old Man
76 says 'The horse beat has ceased. He has ridden
77 round to the back & is putting the horse in
78 He is half drunk, he is always half drunk   sways to & fro
singing about evil
79 the stable She has gone to let him in
boy says he is mad
80 but what does she care she mad about him.
81 He cries out do let him do not let him in
If you do great evil will be done
82 ~~He is evil you are~~ evil ~~Look look there in the~~
83 door. He has taken her in his arms. They are
84 going in—going the marriage bed. ~~Perha~~ Last
85 night—tom night—may be this night I
86 shall be gotten. This night this night.
87 Up there you are about to beget me—I that
88 am the most evil of [?them], this boy that is
89 most evil still— ~~this boy that begot is~~
90 There is a dark evil, a curse that was never
91 broke is born, ~~is~~ begins—it corrupts man after man
~~Th~~
92 woman— He turns to the boy— ~~& pulls him to him~~
93 Old Man says but remains sick that she mar him
94 All her not to—but does not leave his place. He sways
95 while saying it.

---

74 The words in the upper right margin which belong after "there" represent further revisions of the cancelled line.

Lines 76, 77, 79, 81, and 82 were composed in that order, and beginning with l. 76 and ending at l. 79 after "in" following the single quote they are spoken directly by the Old Man. The single quote has been omitted at the end of l. 79. Line 81, which begins with "He cries out," is the narrator's reference to the Old Man; "not" has probably been omitted before the first "let." The single quote and punctuation at the end of the line have been omitted. After writing, cancelling, and revising l. 82, Yeats probably added the three lines that appear opposite l. 78 in the right margin. After having added them, he continued the indirect discourse at the foot of the page. Lines 93–94 contain the Old Man's response to those in the upper right margin, which end with "boy says he is mad." The words that have been inadvertently omitted from l. 93 are "he is not mad" before "but" and a verb such as "told" or "warned" before "her." After Yeats added these lines he probably added ll. 78 and 80 and then drew the directional lines.

79 period omitted after "stable."

82 Possibly a period after "evil."

84 "to" probably omitted before "the."

C

a [illegible] [illegible] — when he
[illegible], & [illegible] his
[illegible] — they are
alone in [illegible]. [illegible] But now she is alone
[illegible] in his [illegible] — [illegible] he is [illegible] her thoughts. The
house [illegible] are [illegible] her thoughts. She died
in giving me birth [illegible] & so does not know that
she has [illegible] — but she knows now — [illegible]
[illegible] She knew he spent all money
on drink, on horses & women — that he never sent me
to school — that I know nothing that I did not pick
up from the workers in the house. [illegible] Then he
spent all — that [illegible] he died a bankrupt, & that
on this night in every year she lives through it all
again & again. She alone in purgatory — he some where
else alone in his. [illegible] Give that
to [illegible] Stop where are you going.
What is that in your hand. You have stolen
my money. You have taken it out of the box.

\6

96 ~~accursed accursed—you & I accursed~~ — ~~what~~ have
97 ~~got there— my money & says they do not~~
98 ~~listen to me—that they cannot me—they~~ are
~~You ar~~
99 alone in ~~the darkness.~~ But now she is alone
100 He is not there — ~~that~~ he is only her thought. The
101 horse beats are only her thought. She died
102 in giving me birth ~~but kn~~ & so did know what
103 she had done—but she knows now—on
104 this ~~night in every year~~ She knew he spent all money
105 & drink & horses & women—that he never sent me
106 to school—that I knew nothing that I did not pick
107 up from the books in the house. ~~Sh knows~~ That he
108 spent all—that ~~That when he~~ he died a bankrupt, & that
109 on this night in every year she lives through it all
110 again & again—she alone in purgatory—he some where
111 ~~else~~ alone in his. ~~What have you got there~~
112 my ~~money—You~~ stop where are you going.
113 What is that in your hands. You have stolen
114 my money You have taken it out of the pack.

---

96 Continues from l. 92 and continues lines that belong to the Old Man. Probably intended to cancel "have."
98 "hear" probably omitted before the second "me"; probably intended to cancel "are."
99 Probably intended to cancel "alone in."
104 Probably intended to cancel "this"; probably intended "knows" here.

7

I did not know why I brought you here — I was un-
sure — but now I know — You are [illegible], [illegible] & beget
children ~~I begot you on a tinker's wench in the~~
~~ditch~~ & there you must die. I begot you on
a tinker's wench in a ditch — but you are no [illegible]
[illegible] — The boy says 'let me go there'
~~Your father~~! He throws the boy down. Your father
burnt the house down in a drunken fury. We were all [illegible]
[illegible] an old half blind servant — I dragged out the
I went for my father but I did not die, then [illegible]
I stabbed him & left him there in the flames. When
I came out my ~~[illegible]~~ hands
were [illegible] my hair was singed, & my ~~[illegible]~~ clothes half burnt off
& [illegible] I [illegible] here ~~[illegible]~~, [illegible] half dead
because I saw [illegible] I saved. [illegible] I [illegible]
There is some one there in the window
~~There they are in the [illegible]~~ [illegible] — The boy
'O my God I [illegible]' You ~~see this~~ can see [illegible]

7

115 I did not know why I brought you here—I was not
116 sure—but now I know— you are young enough to beget
117 children ~~I begot you on a tinkers wench in~~ the
118 ~~ditch, &~~ & there you must die. I begot you on
119 a tinkers wench in a ditch—but you will not beget
120 any body—The boy says 'let me go me go'
121 ~~Your father~~ ' He throws the boy down. Your father
122 burned the house down in a drunken fury. We alone except
123 for an old half blind servant—I dragged out the
124 I went for my father but I did not drag him out
125 I strangled him & left him there in the flames. When
126 I came out my ~~hair was half bu hair & my~~ hands
127 ~~were~~ my hair was singed, & my ~~ha~~ clothes half burned off
128 & they thought I was burned —~~but~~, that was half dead
129 because I had tried to save— Look [?] look
There is some one there in the window
130 ~~There they are in the window~~ again— The boy
can see
131 'O my God my God' You ~~see them~~ now

---

118 Probably intended to cancel second "&."
120 Probably "let" omitted before second "me."
121 The single quote, which is probably cancelled, after "father," encloses words that continue from the preceding line and are spoken by the Boy; "father," at the end of the line should read "grandfather."
122 "were" probably omitted before "alone."
123 "servant" omitted after "the."
128 "I" probably omitted before second "was."

The [illegible] stands there [illegible] in the window, the
can hear [illegible] a tiny head [illegible]. Come
Come - [illegible] his [illegible] this is very [illegible]
She sees. Come come come I say -
[illegible] I may tell, [illegible] my mother [illegible] [illegible] that
the end is finished. ([illegible] and [illegible] [illegible]
[illegible] [illegible] [illegible]) The [illegible] fades [illegible]
is fades the [illegible] back [illegible] again. O my god
[illegible] does not understand - her agony, her agonies [illegible].
[illegible] remorse began all over again. [illegible]
[illegible] [illegible] make see all [illegible]
[illegible] understand that the end is not [illegible] [illegible] finished
O my god what is [illegible]. And the never ends
the misery, the [illegible], & the remorse, the [illegible]

8

he

132 They are standi there ~~side by side~~ in the window; ~~He~~
133 can have ~~no rest~~ a tired beast (~~vision fades). Come~~
134 ~~come—You die for~~ but that is him that is only what
135 she sees. Come come come I say—
136 that I may kill, & my mother find rest know that
137 the evil is finished. (boy rises & comes slowly to
138 Old—who strangles him) The vision fades as
139 it fades the horse beats are heard again. 'O my God
140 she does not understand—her agony, her agonised joy,
141 or her remorse begin all over again. Can
142 ~~you not hear me~~ your spirit mother see all does
143 it understand that the evil it set in motion is finished
144 O my God what is man—Are they never ending
145 the misery of the living & the remorse of the dead

136 "know" probably intended as "knowing."
142–145 Question marks have been omitted after "all," "finished," "man," and "dead."

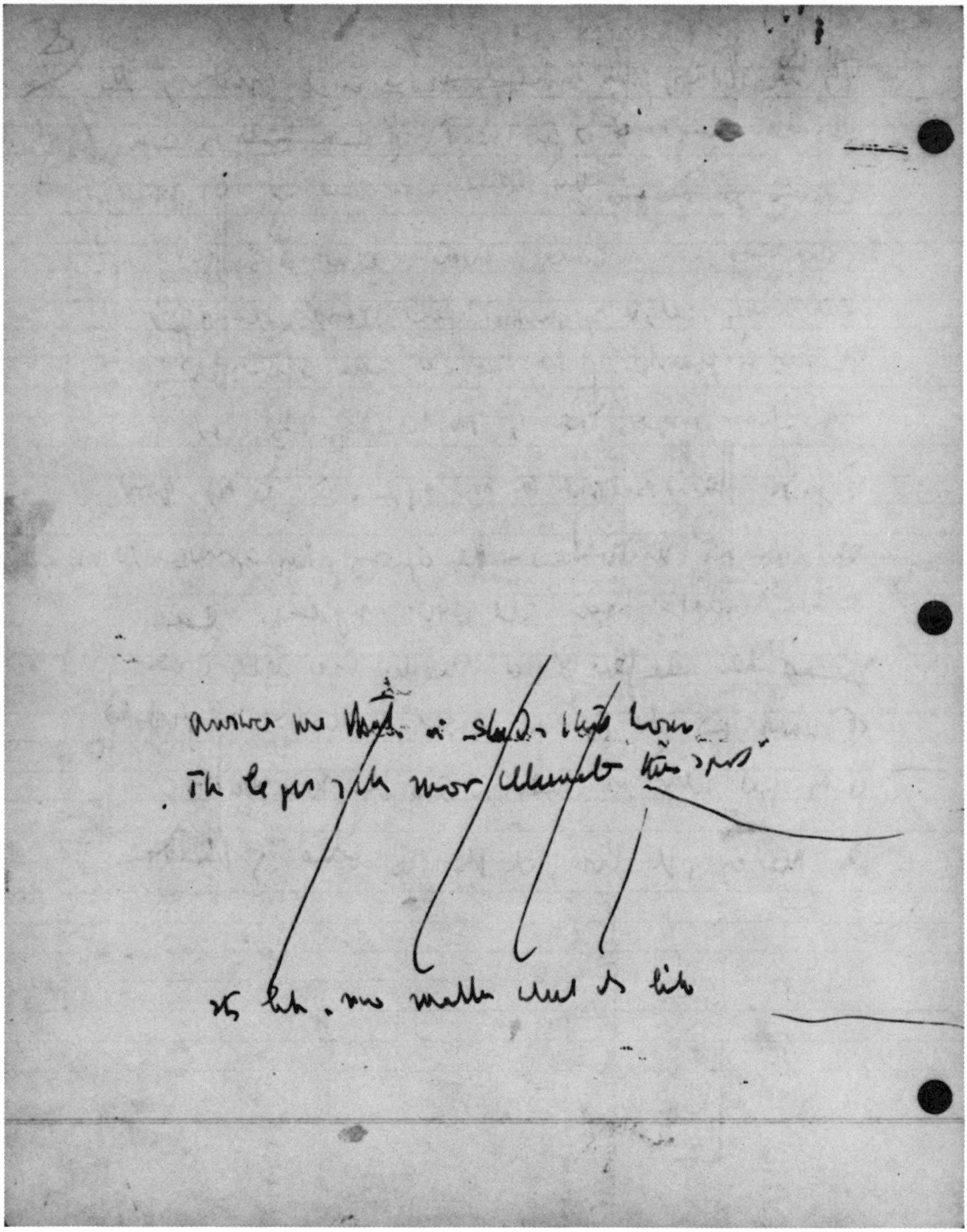

a Answer me that [?] Study that house
b The light of the moon illuminates this spot

c Its like—no matter what its like

P8i^{v} This page, which is written in blue ink, represents a stage of revision intermediary between the first and second verse versions and is reproduced below on p. 73.

Boy: You are trying to [illegible] me.. / more [illegible] [illegible] [illegible]
what you should do now [illegible] / [illegible] [illegible] me.

O M, My mother your grandmother lived in this
house, my ~~mother~~ [illegible] [illegible] [illegible] to

Boy, ~~what is this to be [illegible] me. They are~~ dead
she is dead & she is [illegible]

O M. ~~She is – Ten years ago I came~~ [illegible]

The dead ~~return to the place where~~ they play
in purgatory return to the places where they played
& the places of their happiness – they return again & again

a Boy: You are trying to terrify me. Now you [?~~tefts~~] ter me
b with your stick & now you ~~tef~~ terrify me.
c. OM. My mother your grand mother lived in that
d house.
~~my mother was a high~~ up la
e Boy. ~~What is that to do with me. They are~~ dead
She is dead & she is there
f OM. ~~She is—Ten years ago I came~~ here
g The dead ~~return to the places where~~ they play
h in purgatory rcturn to thc places where they plaid
i to the places of their transgressions—they return again & again

B

O M. It is ten years since I saw this house

B. You have brought me here for some bad reason. I do [illegible]

B. ~~I hate this~~ house — I ~~[illegible]~~ evil
what is this house

O M. It is no worse than any other place — the shadow of the

[illegible] upon it & so [illegible] as it before [illegible] there I

[illegible] [illegible] — one [illegible] fall upon the tree on
[illegible] [illegible] [illegible] [illegible] [illegible]

~~the path [illegible] [illegible]~~ & [illegible] a [illegible] then it [illegible],

B. I hate this tree

O M. It is [illegible] [illegible] [illegible] [illegible] this, the [illegible] [illegible]

[illegible] & it [illegible] like a soul that has passed

[illegible] purgatory

Boy. ~~Why~~ The house is the worse

O M. ~~[illegible]~~ It is not the house [illegible] [illegible] [illegible] [illegible]

[illegible] [illegible] [illegible] [illegible] [illegible] is evil

Boy. Nothing can live but rats & owls. The rafters are black

there is no roof. It must have been burned down

at some time or another.

O M. What drinking & [illegible] [illegible] [illegible] [illegible] [illegible],

two [illegible] [illegible], the [illegible] [illegible] [illegible] [illegible] the

[illegible] [illegible] [illegible] ~~[illegible]~~, [illegible] [illegible] &

& [illegible], [illegible] & [illegible], [illegible] [illegible] ~~[illegible]~~ [illegible]
in the house

B
1 OM. It is ten years since I saw that house
2 B. You have brought me here for some evil reason. I do like that
3 B. ~~I hate that~~ house—it ~~looks to me~~ an evil
4 What is that house
5 OM. It no worse than any other place—the shadow of the
6 falls upon it & so you see it between two streams of
falls where we are one that
7 bright moonlight—one ~~that~~ falls upon that tree one
8 ~~that falls where we are~~ & here a [?] there it [?] evil,
9 B. I hate that tree
10 OM. It is glittering white like some thing that has been
11 purified of its sins like a soul that has passed
12 from purgatory
13 Boy. ~~Why~~ The house is the house
14 OM. ~~You say~~ It is not the house but living in it &
15 lives in it still that is evil
16 Boy. Nothing can live but bats and owls. The rafters ~~are~~ black
17 there is no roof. It must have been burned down
18 at some time or another.
19 OM. What destroys & destroys you me who made ~~us~~
20 two evil brutes; [?] sent us out to walk the
21 roads in poverty ~~[?but] born there,~~ selling needles &
22 & threads, ~~spolls &~~ pins & spools of ~~thread~~ [?even] ~~tho bo~~ this
is the house

Revisions of P1^{r}, intermediary between the scenario and the first verse version, composed during the writing of the scenario or after having completed it.

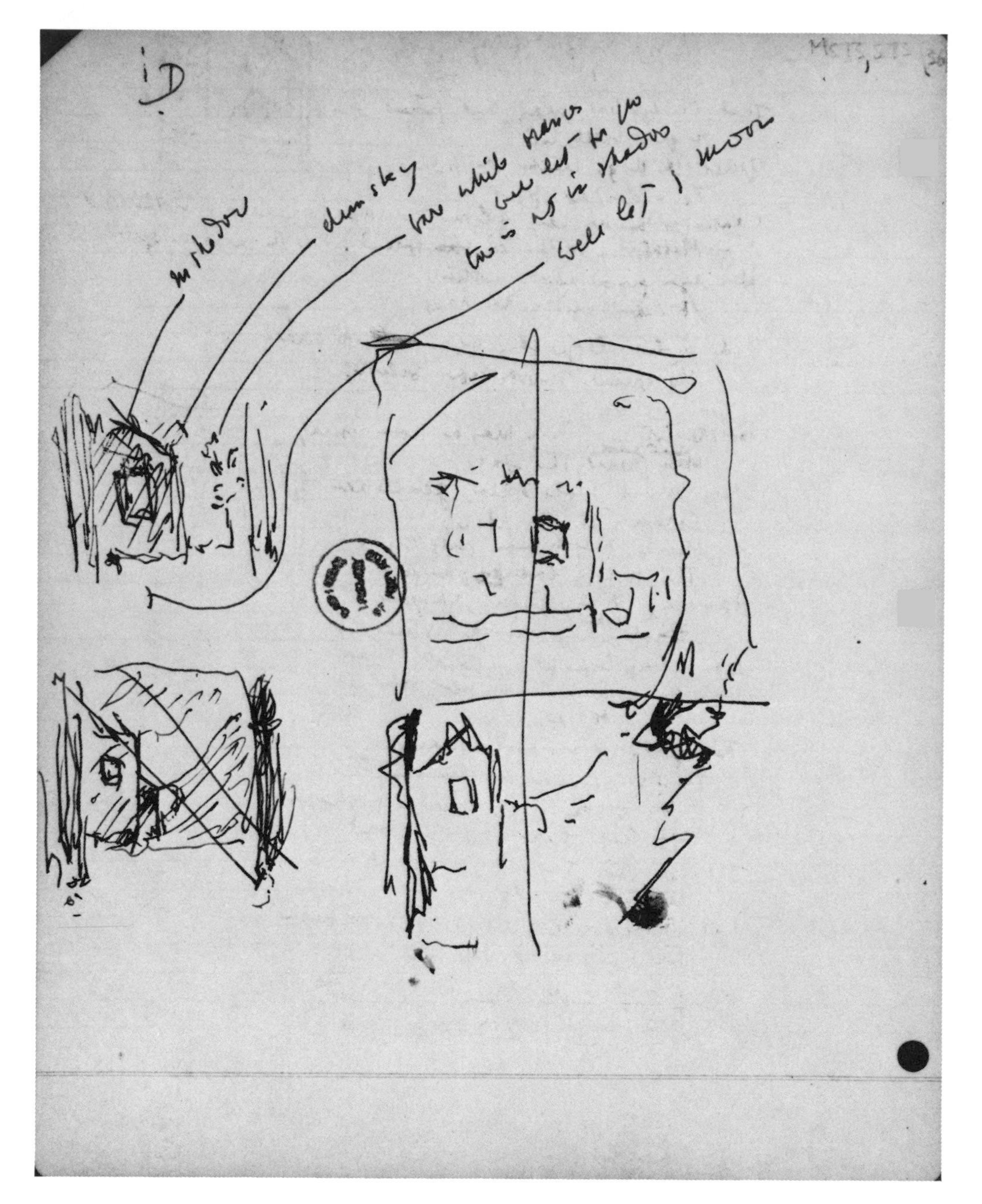

The four directional lines in the upper left corner of page S1^v are followed from left to right by the words:

In shadow

dim sky

bare white branches
well lit for the
tree is not in shadow

well lit by moon

The stage set of *Purgatory*, which Yeats sketched before or after he completed the scenario. The prose transcription above follows the directional lines drawn on the sketch.

Manuscripts of the First Verse Draft: *Purgatory*

MS 8772#2, begun in late March or early April, represents the earliest stage of verse composition. Yeats revised, usually on the verso of the preceding page, either as he composed, or after some time had elapsed. Page 4, which is missing, served as the transition between the Old Man's speech about souls returning to familiar spots and the conclusion of his narrative account of the fall of the house from its past greatness. Yeats probably accomplished the transition in MS#2 in much the same way as he did in MS #3: in the later version the Boy's incredulity provokes the Old Man's anger. But the Old Man's anger is subdued in the process of recounting the history of the house. Since VA5^{r} contains a continuation of that account, we might suppose that Yeats began on the missing page VA4^{r} as he does in the parallel passage in the second verse draft:

Study that house
That is the house where . . .   [MS 8771 VB2^{v}, ll. 8–9]

He begins to recount the history with his own birth, moves imaginatively back in time, and then moves forward to the present. He concludes with his "declaration" speech:

to kill a house
Where great men grew up
married died
offence
I here declare a capital crime.   [MS 8771#2 VA5^{r}, ll. o–r]

The second, revised edition, is only slightly different:

~~murder~~
to kill a house
Where great men grew up, married, died died
~~[?is]~~
I here declare∧a capital offence   [MS 8771#3 VB5^{r}, ll. 10–12]

The topical sequences in MSS#2 and #3 are sufficiently parallel that the missing page

VA6 is likely to have contained the transition that linked the declaration speech and the Old Man's account of the murder of his father. We might expect that the missing leaf contains the Boy's response to the Old Man's declaration speech: the continuation of the Old Man's narrative account, first of how his father deprived him of an education, then of his mother's death. In MS#3, and, probably, in MS#2, the Boy sees his own life mirrored in his father's account of his own past. The history of the one becomes the history of the other. The Old Man's narrative of his father—the Boy's grandfather—follows on VA7^r of MS#2.

The verso of VA7 bears directional lines that do not connect with any extant leaf; however, the page that I have identified as VA9^r contains exactly those passages one would expect to find on the leaf with which VA7 would connect. It is likely that there was an intermediary leaf, VA8, the contents of which were transferred to a fresh leaf. Yeats inscribed in the upper right margin one number that appears to be a mirror image of "9" and another that might be an "8." Because the verso of this leaf connects with the recto of VA10, I have assigned to it the number VA9^r.

Page VA13i^r is an odd leaf which is intermediary between VA12^r, VA13^r, and VA14^r, and is written in black rather than blue-black ink. Yeats probably wrote "14" on the upper right margin because the first line at the head of the page corresponds to the first line on page 14 of MS#2. He then cancelled "14" and renumbered the page "13" after or before he transferred the revised passage to a new page, which followed VA12^r of MS#2 and which he numbered "13." At some time, either before or after he transferred the revised passage, he cancelled the revised passage.

Purgatory

Boy

I am tired of dragging this old pack [illegible]

Old man

[illegible]

Boy

[illegible]

See back

The full moon

1 ~~[?The]~~ hall doors, half doors, front doors, back doors
2 Here & there up down 1
Purgatory
Boy
and
3 I am tired of dragging this old pack ~~about~~
4 ~~[? ? ?] half doors, back~~ doors
[? ?]
5 ~~At night doors, half doors, back doors shuffling my feet~~ to hall doors & half doors
6 Hearing you ~~took~~ talk upon the turn of the path
my mind
ward
Old Man went back∧forty years & more
rose up
7 When this house ~~came in sight~~
~~Before my~~
8 ~~To what it was my memory went back for forty years~~ years
Back
9 Or ~~fifty~~ to the stories of this house
10 I tried to remember what a ~~drunken~~ butler
on ~~upon~~
11 Said to ~~a gamekeeper∧October [?the] first~~ said [?] to a drunken gamekeeper
12 Before my mother had grown ~~to be a lov up~~ to be a woman
and none living can
13 But I could not & ~~no man living can~~ ~~none living~~ has (see back
14 ~~The stories are all dead & the house is dead~~
15 Where are the stories when ~~the stones are taken~~ the threshold
16 ~~To patch a pigsty or to mend a road~~
Patches
17 To patch a pigsty— ~~there is a dead house~~ ~~that house is dead~~
18 My father, he that was your grandfather
See back
19 ~~He that was all evil~~
20 ~~Killed it Killed it~~—I
21 Murdered it—I passed his ~~begetting~~ begetting on
~~Here~~ Where
22 Here ~~stand an~~ evil man & evil boy.
Boy
23 Stop lying—I never asked to see ~~that house~~ it
And it
24 ~~& it must be near upon midnight~~.
Old Man
25 The full moon

Lines 1–2 are revisions of ll. 4–5.
12 "lov" was cancelled before rather than after "to be a" and "up."
24 "it" was cancelled separately before the entire line was cancelled.

Said to a drunken game keeper
But would not of him buy car [illegible] of a horse
When all the [illegible] stories ~~when the [illegible] of the house~~
~~Have gone to pale or some fugitive~~
When the household is gone to [illegible] a fugitive
Answer me that — my fathers boy
He that has your grandfather
Murdered the house & now we come
And evil men an evil boy

Boy
Stop lying [illegible] the [illegible] [illegible] her

Old man
In the light of the full moon

Boy
Stop lying.

Old man
Th of the full moon

But I can tell you
What this murder [illegible] [illegible] [illegible]

1 Said to a drunken gamekeeper
2 But could not & none living can
jokes & of a house
3 Where are the ^ stories ~~when the threshold~~ ~~of the house~~
4 ~~Has gone to patch some pigsty~~
5 When the threshold s gone to patch a pig sty
6 Answer me that—my fathers boy
7 He that was your grandfather
8 Murdered this house & now we come
9 And evil man as evil boy
Boy
10 Stop lying did you bring me here
Old Man
11 The light of the full moon
Boy
12 Stop lying.
Old Man
13 The of the full moon
14 But I can tell you
15 What this thunder riven tree is like

9 ''as'' probably intended as ''and.''
Lines 1–15 are revisions of VA1^{r} ll. 11–25.
13 ''light'' probably omitted after ''the.''

2

Boy

You thought [illegible] that I might have ears to tell

[illegible] always [illegible]

Old man

The first [illegible]

[illegible] a century [illegible]

Illuminate this spot [illegible]

The shadow of the [illegible] upon the [illegible]

And that's symbolical [illegible] stands the [illegible]

[illegible]

Boy

A silly old man.

Old man

A year ago I saw it — shape [illegible]

But the forty years ago I saw [illegible] like [illegible]

[illegible]

[illegible]

The [illegible]

What [illegible]

Boy

[illegible]

Old man

That tree is like the soul in the house

[illegible]

These shadows [illegible]

[illegible]

[illegible]

Past [illegible] the [illegible]

[illegible] Look now the [illegible]

Boy

The [illegible] No [illegible]

[illegible] when [illegible]

What can I say about the house

Before the thunderbolt [illegible]

Green leaves, ripe leaves, leaves [illegible]

[illegible]

Boy

[illegible]

You [illegible]

I am [illegible]

[illegible]

That I may [illegible]

[illegible]

[illegible]

2

Boy
1 You brought me here that I might hear you talk
2 And it is almost midnight
Old Man
3 The full moon
you and a certain tree
4 Illuminates this spot & ~~that old tree and yonder~~ tree
~~is~~ falls
5 The shadow of the hill upon the house
but
6 And that's symbolical ^ study that tree
7 ~~And tell me what's like~~ what is it like
Boy
8 A silly old man.
Old Man
9 A year ago I saw it—striped & bare ~~it was~~
10 ~~But~~ And forty years ago I saw ~~[? ?] the leaves~~ that tree
11 ~~With boughs~~
to
12 ~~Clung like fat butter upon~~ the [?] twigs
13 That was before the lightning struck it
14 What is it like answer me that
Boy
leave me alone
15 ~~How do I know~~
Old Man
16 That tree is like the soul of a woman
17 Half purified in purgatory
that shadow
18 There shadow on it ~~[?]~~ moon light
19 Cold sweet glistening light
~~But what house—there~~
20 ~~But all the house is shaddow~~
at
21 Put down that pack stand in the door
22 ~~Look up—look now—son what~~ is that
23 ~~Look~~ Look now theres some one in the house
Boy
24 The ~~floor has all been burned away~~ No one—the floors have gone
25 ~~The roofs half gone from~~ And where there should be roof ~~but~~ theres sky
26 What can I say about that house

---

18 The indecipherable word is possibly "but"; if so, it is more than likely that "is no" has been omitted before "shadow."

22 "son" possibly intended as "say."

26 This line was probably added after rather than before ll. a–m and is a revision of l. 20, which was then cancelled.

2

Boy

You thought [illegible] [illegible] [illegible] I [illegible] here [illegible] tell

[illegible] is always [illegible]

Old Man

The [illegible] [illegible] years at a certain [illegible]

I [illegible] this spot [illegible] [illegible] [illegible] [illegible] [illegible]

The shadow of the [illegible] [illegible] the house

And that is symbolical [illegible] [illegible] [illegible] [illegible]

[illegible] [illegible] [illegible] [illegible] [illegible]

Boy

A silly old man.

Old M

A year ago I saw it — [illegible] [illegible] [illegible]

But [illegible] forty years ago I saw [illegible] [illegible] [illegible]

[illegible]

[illegible] [illegible] [illegible] [illegible] the [illegible]

That [illegible] [illegible] [illegible] [illegible] [illegible]

What [illegible] [illegible] [illegible] [illegible] [illegible] [illegible] [illegible]

Boy

[illegible] [illegible] [illegible]

[illegible] [illegible] [illegible]

Before the [illegible] [illegible] [illegible] [illegible]

[illegible] [illegible], [illegible] [illegible], [illegible] [illegible] [illegible] [illegible]

[illegible] [illegible] [illegible] [illegible] [illegible] [illegible]

Boy

[illegible] [illegible] [illegible]

You [illegible] [illegible] [illegible] [illegible]

I [illegible] [illegible] [illegible]

[illegible] [illegible] [illegible] [illegible] [illegible]

That I [illegible] [illegible] [illegible] you [illegible]

[illegible] [illegible] [illegible]

[illegible] [illegible] [illegible]

[illegible] [illegible] [illegible] [illegible]

[illegible] [illegible] [illegible] [illegible] [illegible]

Old Man

[illegible] [illegible] [illegible] The [illegible] [illegible] [illegible] [illegible]

[illegible] [illegible] [illegible] [illegible]

[illegible] [illegible] [illegible] [illegible] [illegible] [illegible]

[illegible] [illegible] [illegible] [illegible]

[illegible] [illegible] [illegible] [illegible] [illegible]

[illegible] [illegible] [illegible] [illegible] [illegible] [illegible]

Put down the pack [illegible] [illegible] [illegible]

[illegible] [illegible] [illegible] [illegible] [illegible] [illegible] [illegible] [illegible]

[illegible] [illegible] [illegible] [illegible] [illegible] [illegible] [illegible] [illegible]

Boy

The [illegible] [illegible] [illegible] [illegible] [illegible] [illegible] No [illegible] — the [illegible] [illegible] [illegible]

[illegible] [illegible] [illegible] [illegible] [illegible] [illegible] [illegible] [illegible] [illegible] [illegible] [illegible] [illegible]

What can I say about the house

riven
~~stricken~~
a Before the thunderbolt ~~[?]~~ had ~~struck~~ it
~~thick~~
b Green leaves, ripe leaves, leaves ~~fat~~ as butter
c ~~Clung to the twigs~~ greasy life, thick as butter
Thick
Boy
d ~~Its almost midnight~~
e ~~You ve dragged~~ here
f I am dragged here
g ~~Always it must [?be] on midnight~~
h That I may listen to you talk
And
i Its almost midnight
Old Man
j What is that tree
~~Study that tree~~
What
k stet ~~What is it like~~—answer me that
Boy
l Leave me alone
Old Man
What is it like
m ~~That tree is~~ like

---

a–m After Yeats reached l. 15 he began to revise in the right margin rather than on the verso of VA1^{v}, which already contained revisions. Lines a–c are revisions of ll. 11–14; l. f is a revision of ll. d–e; and l. f and ll. h–i replace l. 15. Rather than resume at l. 16, he added ll. j–m, which are new lines. After having added them in the right margin, he began to move the new lines he wished to retain to the center of the page to become ll. 14–15 and cancelled ll. j–l. He neither transferred nor cancelled l. m. It is possible that once he continued with l. 16, which answers the question l. m poses, there was no need to retain it, although he neglected to cancel the line.

a Answer me that [?] Study that house
b The light of the moon illuminates this spot

c Its like—no matter what its like

1 If upon others others may ~~bring~~ help
2 For when the ~~con~~ consequences end
3 The dream should, if upon them selves
4 There help in god

Boy
Those books you read
5 ~~Books that you read~~ ~~Because of the~~ books
6 ~~Before you grow to be a~~
7 When you were but a lad & knew no better
8 Have left you but a silly old man

1–4 These are revisions of VA3^{r}, ll. 9–13; either an apostrophe ''s'' or ''is'' probably intended after ''There''; the line should be read as: ''There is no help but in God.''

5–8 These are revisions of VA3^{r}, ll. 4–6; the mark after ''a'' is probably an ink blot.

8

and here a bit of an egg shell thrown
out of a starling's or jackdaw's nest

Old M

~~Souls in purgatory [illegible] this [illegible] years ago~~
~~[illegible] their [illegible] a year [illegible] [illegible]~~
The souls of purgatory are in these houses
A certain care [illegible] at the window

~~[illegible]~~
~~That~~ a year ago — this [illegible] year
~~The souls of~~ souls in purgatory [illegible] [illegible]
To [illegible] a particular spot
~~[illegible]~~
Go there their thoughts [illegible] transgression
Again & again plunging at last
What are their consequences [illegible]
Have helped others or when these [illegible]

Boy

The tales you tell when you are young
~~Tell them [illegible] [illegible] in the house~~
And left you but a silly old man

Old Man

How [illegible] or [illegible] or [illegible].
This is the point, can you not see it boy
If upon others ~~[illegible]~~ we can help
[illegible] the [illegible] here
[illegible] suppose [illegible]
[illegible] of upon these souls what help
Can the living offer [illegible] the point.

Boy

3

1 And heres a bit of an egg shell thrown
2 Out of a stares, or jackdaws nest
Old M
3 ~~Soul in purgatory was there a year ago~~
4 ~~And will be there again to night~~
5 The souls of purgatory are in that house
at
6 A couple came & stood in the window
7 ~~One & then one~~
8 ~~That~~ A year ago—there in it yet
all
9 ~~The souls in~~ souls in purgatory ~~retr~~ come back
10 To habitations & familiar spots
11 ~~And live through old~~
12 And there live through their old transgressions
13 Again & again & knowing at last
14 What ever evil consequence their acts
15 Have had upon others or upon themselves
Boy
16 The books you read when you were young
17 ~~Put all~~ Have put nonsense in your head
18 And left you but a silly old man
Old Man
19 Have had on others or themselves.
20 This is the point, can you not see it boy
21 If upon others ~~I can bring them peace~~ we can help
22 For when the consequences here
23 End suffering there must end
24 But if upon them selves what help
25 Can the living offer resolve the past.
Boy

After l. 2 the mark before "M" is probably an ink blot.
25 "to" probably omitted after "offer."

5

Old Man

1 ~~He got her spend all she had~~
2 He got her & the house is dead
3 Great people had been born there
4 ~~Magistrates & Colonels & the~~ like
5 Members of parliament & long ago
6 A man that fought in Sarsfields army
7 Those that went far came to die
8 Or came in spring to look at the may flowers
9 ~~They loved that house &~~ the great trees
10 Those that far away
11 Those ~~went that were in government~~ went
12 To London and India came home to die
13 Or came to see the may flowers in the park
14 They loved the passages of the house
15 And loved the trees but he spent all
16 ~~Drink women dice the lord knows~~ what
17 On women horses drink & dice
18 She did not the worst because
19 She died in giving birth to me
a soul
20 But now ~~being~~ in purgatory
~~and so suffers~~
21 She knows it all. ~~She knows it all~~ s
she knows it all
22 ~~He tried to keep me ignorant~~
23 To ~~keep me on his own level but~~ some
24 He thought to keep me on his ~~lv~~ level
25 ~~Refusing~~ Refused me education but some

Colonels
a Magistrates, members of parliament,
Captains & governors &
b ~~Colonels & capitins &~~ long ago
c A general that fought at ~~Oc~~ Aughrim
d Some that had gone on government work
e To London or to India came home to die
f Or came from London every spring
bloom
g To see the May flower in the park
h ~~They loved the passages~~ of the house
i And loved the trees that he cut down
j ~~To furnish him with horses~~
k To pay for what he lost on cards
~~[?he] loved~~
l Or ~~pa~~ spent on horses women ~~drink~~ drink
the intricate
m ~~They loved~~ ^ ~~the~~ ^ passages of the house
n Then he killed house and all
o to kill a house
p Where great men grew up
q married died
offence
r I here declare a capital crime.
s My mother never knew the worst

The preceding page, which is lost, is discussed in the introductory note to MS 8771#2.
18 "know" probably omitted after "not."
a–s These lines are revisions of ll. 4–18.

[illegible]

[illegible] [illegible] [illegible] [illegible]

~~[illegible] [illegible] [illegible] [illegible]~~

~~[illegible] [illegible] [illegible] [illegible]~~

Boy

Not to [illegible] father

[illegible] his body [illegible] on his [illegible]

Boy

Not to father — I ~~stagger~~ [illegible]

Then dragged her out [illegible] help.

~~That I [illegible] [illegible] [illegible] [illegible]~~

~~[illegible] [illegible] [illegible] [illegible] [illegible] dead~~

~~[illegible] [illegible] [illegible] [illegible]~~

~~[illegible] [illegible] [illegible] [illegible] there~~

I [illegible] [illegible]

~~And dragged [illegible] from the burning~~ [illegible]

As dragging her [illegible] the [illegible] flame

[illegible] dragged her out [illegible]

Drew [illegible] up the [illegible]

I [illegible] a [illegible]

~~[illegible] [illegible] [illegible] after [illegible]~~

Because [illegible] [illegible] [illegible] [illegible]

And all that dragged her [illegible] [illegible]

The dragged her out ~~[illegible] [illegible]~~ [illegible] [illegible]

~~[illegible] [illegible] [illegible] [illegible]~~ [illegible]

~~The [illegible] [illegible] [illegible] [illegible] [illegible]~~

The [illegible] [illegible] [illegible] [illegible] [illegible]

~~[illegible]~~ The body [illegible] [illegible] [illegible] [illegible]

Z

Father
1 Is there nobody in ear shot
2 ~~My eyes begin to age~~
3 Your eyes are young
Boy
4 Nobody father
there
5 Is^no body but our two selves
Boy
6 Nobody father—I ~~strangled him~~
7 Then dragged him out & made believe
stet
8 That I had saved him from the fire
W
9 Shen somebody found out that he was dead
10 I wept & wailed, then somebody
11 Found finger marks upon his throat
12 ~~I wept and writhed~~
13 ~~And dragged him from the burning~~ stair
14 And dragged him amidst the ~~fule~~ flames
15 Somebody dragged him out & somebody
16 Discovered finger upon his throat
17 I drove a knife
18 ~~Between his ribbs & after that~~
19 Between his third & second ribs
20 And after that dragged him in the fire
21 They dragged him out ~~all charred & black &~~ somebody saw
22 ~~[? ? ?] knife [? ? ?] done~~
23 ~~The rent my knife had made but was not sure~~
he
24 The knife wound but^was not sure
25 ~~[?]~~ The body was all black & charred

The preceding page, which is lost, is discussed in the introductory note to MS 8771#2.
16 "marks" probably omitted after "finger."
22 The cancelled indecipherable word is possibly the first three letters of "Because."

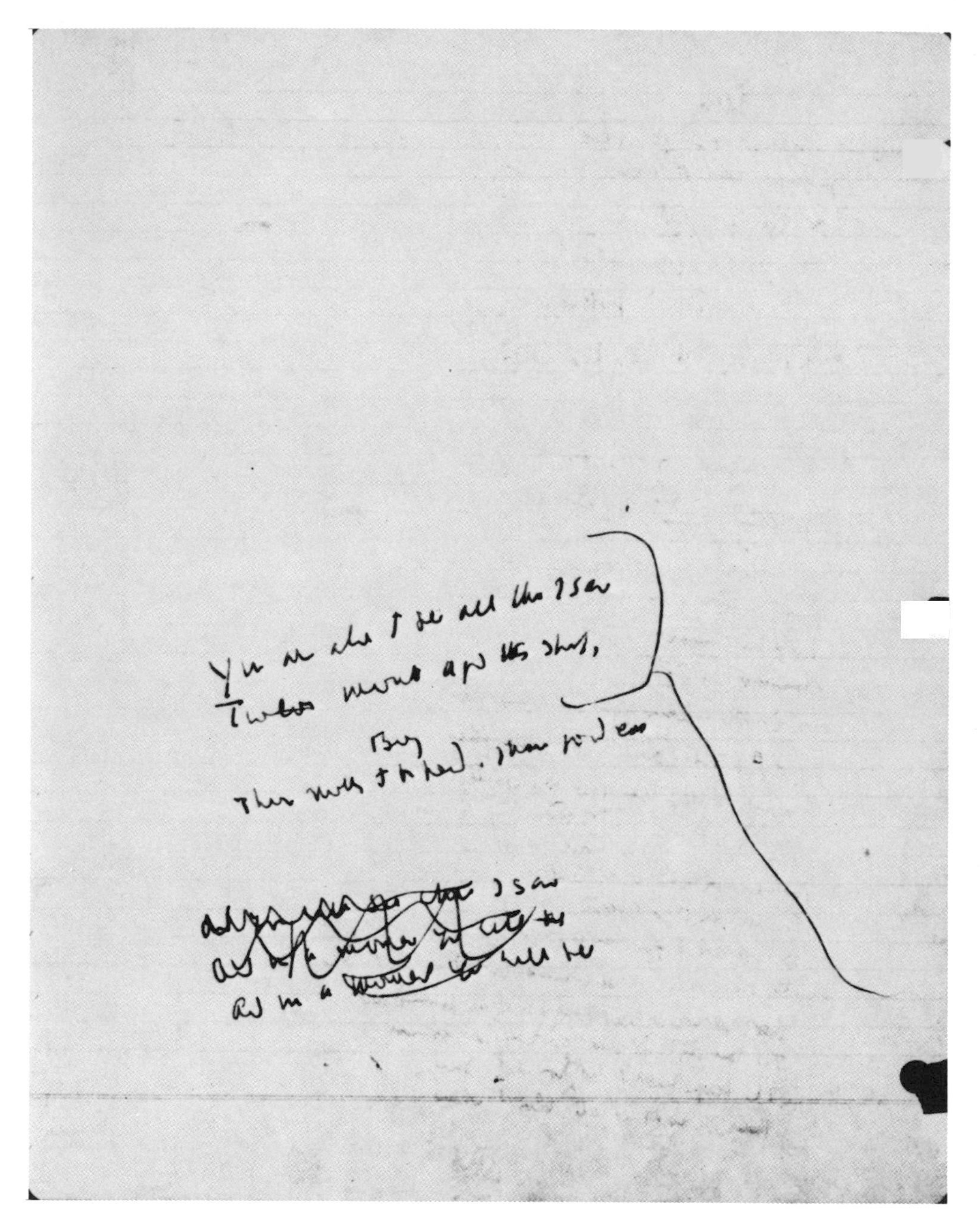

1 You are about to see all that I saw
2 Twelve months ago this spot.
Boy
3 Theres nothing to be heard. I have good ears

4 ⌈And you will see what I saw
5 | And in a moment you will ~~see~~
6 ⌊And in a moment you will see

The leaf with which the directional lines on this page connect is missing. The description of the ghosts of the Old Man's mother and father, which the missing VA8r would have contained, appears on VA9r. Directional lines on VA9v connect with VA10r.

5 "see" was cancelled separately, before the entire passage was cancelled.

Old Man

[illegible]

My father is ready for the [illegible] public house

He [illegible] a whiskey bottle under his arm —

drunk at the window [illegible] — she [illegible]

Lesley — the servants are all in bed

She is alone [illegible] stage is

[illegible] drinks at public house

Boy

No the window is quite dark

You have made it up — no you are mad

And getting madder, every day madder

Father

The [illegible] because they have

[illegible] upon a gravelled avenue

[illegible] a gravelled avenue

[illegible] grass

Where there is

They [illegible] on a gravelled avenue

[illegible] — [illegible]

[illegible]

[illegible] [illegible]

[illegible] — [illegible]

[illegible] To [illegible] the horse [illegible]

She has gone down to open the door

He is half [illegible]

[illegible] down

What does it matter, that he is half dead

[illegible] on they

That night she is [illegible]

He is half drunk [illegible]

Old Man

~~Horse hoffs~~ ~~those horse hoofs boy~~ e 7

1 My father is riding from the ~~tavern~~ public house
2 He ~~has a bottle of~~ ~~whiskey under~~ a whiskey bottle under his arm—
3 Look at the window ~~she is standing there~~—she stands there

all

4 Listening—the servants are^in bed
5 She is alone. He has staggered in
6 Bragging & drinking the public house

Boy

No

7 ~~no body~~ the window is quite dark
8 You have made it up—no you are ~~mad~~ mad
9 And getting mader, every day mader

Father

~~now~~

10 The hoofs are louder ~~now~~ because they beat
11 ~~Although the avenue is all gravel to day~~

upon a gravelled avenue

12 ~~He rides on gravel~~
13 ~~He upon a gravelled~~ avenue
14 ~~Where now there is only~~ grass
15 Where there is
16 They beat upon a gravelled avenue

Where grass grows now I

17 ~~Though its all grass today~~ — ~~use~~ hear & see
18 ~~Wh she heard forty years ago~~
19 What her mind hears & sees
20 He has ~~stopped now~~ stopped—gone to the other side
21 ~~To put his horse in the stable~~ To put his horse at the stable
22 She has gone down to open the door

~~cares~~

23 ~~He is~~ half ~~drunk but what can she she used but what can she~~
24 [~~What matter that he is half~~ drunk
25 ~~What does it matter that he is half~~ drunk
26 ~~Well matched are they~~]
27 This night she is no better than her man
28 He is half drunk but she is mad about him.

Below the letter "e" there is a vertical line that resembles the number "1" but does not appear to be of any significance.

18 The unformed word is probably the beginning of "what."

23 "she used" was probably cancelled before Yeats cancelled the entire line; changing the second "can" to "cares" opened the possibility of blaming the mother as well as the father for the "fall" of the house.

24 probably intended to cancel "drunk."

[illegible] [illegible]
O mother of the [illegible] [illegible]
Of the [illegible] [illegible] [illegible] the [illegible] [illegible]
And I the [illegible], it is not [illegible]
That drunken man came [illegible]
O mother I must not be born
The man you carry in your womb
A miserable man sunk in poverty
An evil man & the [illegible] ; [illegible]
Remember if he beget one he begets
Her murderer. O my God
She cannot hear ~~[illegible]~~ the door is shut
And ~~[illegible] [illegible] [illegible]~~
~~That [illegible]~~
And she is locked into a dream
~~[illegible] [illegible] [illegible] [illegible] [illegible] [illegible]~~
I ~~[illegible]~~ [illegible]
I [illegible] I have forgotten. [illegible]
If I lay hand upon your ~~[illegible]~~ shoulder
I may remember that I live
~~[illegible] [illegible] [illegible]~~ And that alone or seen the [illegible]
That [illegible] in sleep [illegible]

come near you
1 O mother do him ~~touch~~ you
2 If he comes near you he will touch
3 And I be gotten, it is not true
4 That drunken men cannot beget
5 O mother I must not be born
6 Nor must you carry in your womb
7 A miserable man sunk in poverty
8 An evil man & the polution of your blood
9 Remember if he begets me he begets
10 His murderer. O my God
11 She cannot hear ~~the lock is turned~~ the door is shut
12 And though there ~~seems to be but glass between~~
13 ~~That glass is there~~
14 And she is locked into a dream
15 ~~Boy if I put my hand upon your shoulder~~
I ~~may remember~~
16 I mad & have forgotten, Boy
17 If I lay hand upon your ~~should~~ shoulder
18 I may remember that I live
glass
19 ~~And yet unborn~~ ~~Although un~~born And that although it seems but^gl
20 That window is deaf too

1 "not let" probably omitted after "do".

20

~~She does not [illegible] [illegible]~~ call it
She does not know [illegible] I see it
~~[illegible]~~
In the [illegible] now. ~~[illegible]~~ They move to this
She brings him into her own chamber / into the marriage chamber — now
The window is dimly lighted ~~[illegible]~~
~~Because she has [illegible] the [illegible] [illegible]~~ [illegible] chamber
~~Because the [illegible] door is open~~
Because ~~[illegible]~~ she has put the candle in the [illegible]
~~[illegible] chamber door is open~~
And the passage door is open. Now
The door is closed the window darks
~~O mother [illegible]~~ I [illegible] [illegible] news
Mother [illegible] [illegible] it is not true
That drunken men cannot beget
Do not permit him to beget on [illegible]
~~I am an [illegible]~~
~~Do not [illegible] [illegible] [illegible] murder~~
A mindless man, ~~[illegible]~~, to [illegible], [illegible]
A wild man [illegible] blood, pollution
Remember, that if ~~he beget [illegible] a [illegible]~~ beget me, he beget
[illegible] and that you must bear
~~The [illegible] [illegible] [illegible]~~ murderer
O my [illegible] you came here and the [illegible]
Shut up ~~[illegible]~~ in her own ~~[illegible]~~ [illegible] you dream,
I am mad to think she could hear
Boy, if I put my hand upon your shoulder
I may know that I am a living man
That many years has passed since this [illegible]
~~That [illegible] [illegible]~~
~~That [illegible] [illegible] is [illegible] this has happened always~~
What [illegible] now has happened always

10

1 ~~She do not know she does not~~ care if

2 She does not know care care I see it

~~I see them~~

3 In the eye of the mind. ~~Sh~~ They mount the stairs

her

4 She brings him into her own chamber < Into the marriage chamber—now

5 The window is dimly light now up

6 ~~Because she has put the candle on the table~~

~~that chamber~~

7 ~~Because the bedroom door is open~~

8 Because ~~And~~ she has put the candle on the table

That chamber

9 ~~And the bed room door is open~~

10 And the passage door is open. Now

11 The door is closed the window dark

12 O mother mother do let him near

13 Nor touch you for it is not true

14 That drunken men cannot beget

15 Do not permit him to g beget me

16 ~~I am an evil man~~

17 Do not ~~permit him to beget~~ his murderer

18 A miserable man, ~~wet road, to~~ wear, wet road

19 An evil man & your blood's polution

he is

20 Remember that ~~if he begets me a begotten~~ begets me, he begets

His murderer & that you must bear

21 ~~He begets & you must bear~~ his murderer

22 O my god you cannot hear

locked up & the locked turned

23 Shut ~~up & locked in her own dream~~ into your dream

24 I am mad to think she could hear

25 Boy if I put my hand upon your shoulder

26 I may know that I am a living man

27 That many years have passed between there & here

28 ~~That nothing can be~~ changed

29 ~~That everything that is future there has happened already~~

30 What future there has happened already

---

2 "if" probably omitted after the first "care"; the second "care" and the word "know" were retained by mistake.

5 "light" probably intended as "lit."

12 "not" probably omitted after "do."

18 The last five words are conjectural.

And here; a problem boy — [illegible] [illegible]
Thought [illegible] in every detail
Compelled to [illegible] remote days
Can the [illegible] of the sequence and
And for our pleasure [illegible] [illegible]
Of pleasure & remorse [illegible] left behind
Where [illegible] is the question? — & look scholarly
Go [illegible] [illegible] [illegible] & I
[illegible] all the problem [illegible]
Which thing is [illegible] me — [illegible]
[illegible]
[illegible]
[illegible]
Father & Son [illegible] [illegible] my [illegible]
[illegible] [illegible] [illegible] [illegible]
Come [illegible]
Come here [illegible] as [illegible] — [illegible]
You have been [illegible] in the [illegible]
[illegible]
[illegible]
You thought I [illegible]
You thought I could not Talk [illegible]
I have [illegible] in the [illegible] — [illegible]
[illegible]
[illegible] [illegible] [illegible]

1 And here's a problem boy—she lives
2 Through everything in exact detail
3 Compelled to it by remorse & yet
she renew
4 Can the ~~renewal~~ of the sexual act
5 And find no pleasure in it & if not
6 If pleasure & remorse must both be there
7 Which is the greater?—I lack schooling
8 Go fetch Turtullian ~~boy~~—he & I
9 Will ravel all that problem out
10 While they're be getting me— ~~come back~~
11 ~~Evil upon evil~~
and so
12 You turned a robber while I talked
and
13 Grandfather^ ~~so~~ ~~father son, evil upon~~ evil
14 Father & son evil after evil and I my self
15 Evil upon evil polution of her blood
here
Come ~~here back~~
~~back~~ here
16 Come ~~here~~ ~~I say~~ and show me—what you have got
17 You have been rumaging in the pack
18 ~~You [th??] I see~~
19 While they
20 ~~You thought I could not talk~~ & see
21 You thought I could not talk & [?see?so]
but
rumaged ~~that~~ it seems^right
22 Have ~~rumaged~~ in the pack— ~~polution~~ ~~is~~ ~~natural~~
23 ~~Re polution~~ ~~Polution robbs pollution~~—
24 Has robbed ~~That polution~~ ~~should rob polution~~

This page is a revised version of VA11^r with which the directional lines connect.
13 "so" probably cancelled separately, before the entire line was cancelled.
18 The indecipherable word is probably "thought"; "could not" was probably omitted after "I."
22 "that it" above "is" probably begun with uppercase letter.

And hear a purple wing
sky
~~Resolve this purple~~ wing. ~~[illegible]~~ lives,
Through everything [illegible] delay
~~[illegible] flowers after~~
~~[illegible] the things [illegible]~~ is
But to [illegible] the things [illegible]
The ~~pleasure of the senses [illegible]~~ compelled by suffering & yes
Crucified ~~by suffering & yes~~ ~~[illegible]~~
relic
Can the leave the senses and
~~[illegible] pleasure [illegible]~~
And find no pleasure [illegible]
Of suffering & pleasure never [illegible] this
What is the greater — ~~[illegible]~~ a purple
~~That [illegible]~~ [illegible] Felt the Turbulent wing,
For I saw it [illegible] the [illegible]
While it was bigger [illegible]

~~[illegible]~~ [illegible] up
~~[illegible]~~ [illegible]
~~[illegible]~~
~~[illegible]~~ [illegible] running in the fields
And [illegible], [illegible]
[illegible]
[illegible] you would [illegible] what I [illegible]
[illegible]
A running [illegible] — [illegible]
~~[illegible]~~ [illegible]
Boy
[illegible]

11

1 And hear a problem boy
She
2 ~~Resolve this problem~~ boy— ~~They~~ lives
3 Through every thing in exact detail
4 ~~But does she live in in her thought alone~~
5 ~~But is that only in her thought, or~~ is
6 But is that in her thought alone or is
7 The ~~pleasure of the sexual act renewed~~
~~to it by su~~ Compelled to it by suffering & yet
8 ~~Compelled by suffering, and yet~~ ~~Compelled to it by remorse~~
relive
9 Can she renew the sexual act
10 ~~Without some pleasure in it~~
11 And find no pleasure it & if not
12 If suffering & pleasure must be there
13 Which is then greater— ~~& heres a thought~~ ~~theres~~ a problem
14 ~~That needs Tur~~ Go f fetch Turtullian boy
15 For I have it solved upon the instant
16 While they are begetting me
17 ~~Come—back, Come back. Pick~~ up
not
18 ~~No—no—no~~ you will not get away
19 ~~So you have been robbing me~~
20 ~~Give~~ So you have been rumaging in the pack
21 And ~~evi~~ robbing
back come back no no
Come back thief ~~No no~~—
22 ~~Come back, come~~ back
23 ~~So~~ you thought you could rob me while I talk
Robbed by that boy
24 And rumagged in the pack— ~~give me~~ that
25 Robbed by my father & my son
26 ~~Pick up those coins,~~ evil upon evil
27 ~~Evil upon evil~~ — polution of her blood
28 Boy ~~She never can have rest~~
29 ~~She cannot rest while it runs on~~
30 ~~Why did I bring him to this house pl~~
31 Why have I brought him to this
32 place she cannot rest while

After composing and revising ll. 1–7, Yeats transferred to VA10v the two lines he wished to retain and cancelled the entire passage. Either before or after he cancelled it, he wrote and revised ll. 8–9, which he revised further. It is likely that after he composed and revised ll. 10–16, he later revised them further as he transferred them to VA10v.

4 "in" after "live" probably intended as "it."

9 "re" has possibly been cancelled.

11 "in" probably omitted after the word "pleasure."

17–22 After composing these lines, Yeats cancelled all but the two-word line "no no" above l. 22, although he probably intended to cancel these words with the others. He transferred "come back" to VA10v, l. 10, but eventually cancelled that line. He also cancelled ll. 11–15, which represents a new version of ll. 23–27, VA11r. He then revised ll. 16–24 further and retained l. 16 but cancelled ll. 17–20. What eventually remained were ll. 21–22.

28–32 These lines are more repetitive and speculative than dramatic and were cancelled in favor of the lines that continue the argument between the Boy and the Old Man on VA12r.

1 Show what you got—Thats [?natural]
2 Thinking I could not talk & see
3 You robbed the pack—wolf robbed ~~wo~~ wolf
4 Polution robbed polution & I
5 Am robbed by father & by son
6 ~~Give~~

Boy

all
7 You kept it∧never gave me a share
8 I will keep it all—you killed by grandad
9 Because you you young & he was old
10 Now I am young and you are old
11 Touch me & I will strangle you
But look ~~lo~~ look it was no lie
12 ~~O my god, my god~~ ~~you were not~~ lying
13 The ~~window is all lighted up~~
14 That upper window is lit up

The directional lines connect with VA12^{r}.
Lines 3–5 are further revision of VA11^{r}, ll. 25–27, which were further revised on 10^{v}, ll. 22–24.
By way of an unexpected conflation of words, the "pack" of money appears to have evoked the word "wolf."

12

[illegible] I keep the [illegible]

~~[illegible]~~

[illegible] give me a [illegible]

[illegible] I keep it all

[illegible] my grand[illegible]

Now [illegible] I am [illegible]

~~[illegible]~~

[illegible] now

[illegible]

[illegible] the window [illegible]

[illegible] my grandad [illegible] the window

[illegible]

Now [illegible] I am [illegible]

O ~~[illegible]~~ [illegible]

[illegible] I [illegible] keep it all.

~~The window~~ [illegible]

~~My grandad [illegible] out of the window~~

[illegible]

[illegible] the window [illegible]

My ~~grand~~ grandad [illegible] the window

[illegible]

12

1 Give me that money

Boy

I keep the money

2 ~~You kept it all~~ I

3 You kept it never gave me a share

now I will keep it all you kept it all

4 ~~And now Illl keep it~~—you kill ~~fath~~ my grand father

5 But you are old & I am young

6 Look there—my god

~~way~~

7 Look there—I go my own ~~p~~ now

8 Let go or I will strangle you

9 ~~O~~ my god—the window is lit

10 ~~It was not~~ lies My grand dad looks out the window

11 For he was old & you were young

12 Now you are old & I am young

13 ~~O my god the window is lit~~ up.

~~And~~

And

14 ~~And~~ I will keep it all.

15 ~~The window is~~ lit

16 My ~~grand dad is looking out of the~~ window

17 ~~You [?]~~ O my God

18 You did lie the window is lighted up

19 My ~~God~~ grand dad is looking out of the window

Old Man

Lines 1–9 were cancelled and replaced with ll. 1–6, VA11v.

4 "my" omitted after "kill" which was probably intended as "killed."

8 As the Old Man, in this version, strangled his father, so the Boy threatens to strangle the Old Man. This line is preserved in the revision on VA11v, l. 11.

10–19 were cancelled and replaced with ll. 7–14, VA11v.

18 "not" probably omitted after "did."

13

Old man

He has come to the [illegible] room to [illegible] a glo[illegible]

A [illegible] heart and where do I [illegible] this word

Then it [illegible] [illegible] fell [illegible] [illegible] A [illegible]

Yet [illegible] nothing in the world nothing

That [illegible] [illegible] [illegible] in [illegible] [illegible]

She is alone in her remorse

That her heart [illegible] knowing nothing

If I should kill a [illegible] under the [illegible]

He would not even [illegible] her head,

[illegible] I [illegible] I get the knife I saw

Boo That in your hand is that [illegible]

O you are [illegible] the [illegible] [illegible]

[illegible] me

[illegible] [illegible] [illegible]

Boo other has [illegible] [illegible]

I am [illegible]

Old man Ty

[illegible] in [illegible] [illegible] [illegible], [illegible] father [illegible]

[illegible] mother [illegible] [illegible] [illegible] [illegible] [illegible]

[illegible] [illegible] is something that I [illegible] [illegible] [illegible]

~~[illegible] I [illegible]~~ [illegible]

If I say it [illegible] to [illegible] my mother

I have no words — dear mother

Because I have [illegible] all that [illegible]

The [illegible] empty [illegible] [illegible] [illegible]

I kill [illegible] [illegible] because it [illegible] [illegible]

13

Old Man

1 He has come to the front room to find ~~[?the]~~ a gla
2 A tired beast ~~[?and]~~ Where did I read these words
3 Then the bride sleep fell upon ~~Adam~~ Adam
is
4 Yet there nothing in the window nothing
5 But the impression upon my mothers mind
6 She is alone in her remorse
7 That tired beast there knowing nothing
8 If I should kill a man under the window
9 He would not even turn his head
10 Father & son & yet the knife the same
11 That is your heart—that finishes
Bo
12 O you are not That stabs boys
Old Man
13 Ah ah ~~[?at]~~ ~~[?ah]~~
Boy
[?] has finished me
14 I ~~am finished~~
Old Man
Thy
15 Hush a by ~~[b?]~~ baby your fathers a knight
16 Thy mother a lady lovely & bright
17 No that is something that I read in book
18 ~~It is my mother I would sing~~
19 If I sing it must be for my mother
And the
20 ^I have not words—Dear mother
21 Because I have finished all that evil
22 The window empty sink into your peace
23 I killed that lad because he had youth

---

10 Possibly the stroke that is transcribed as "the" is intended as an apostrophe followed by the letter "s" and has been detached from the word "knife." If so, "the" has been inadvertently omitted.

12 "That stabs the boy" is the continuation of ll. 10–11 and belongs to the Old Man.

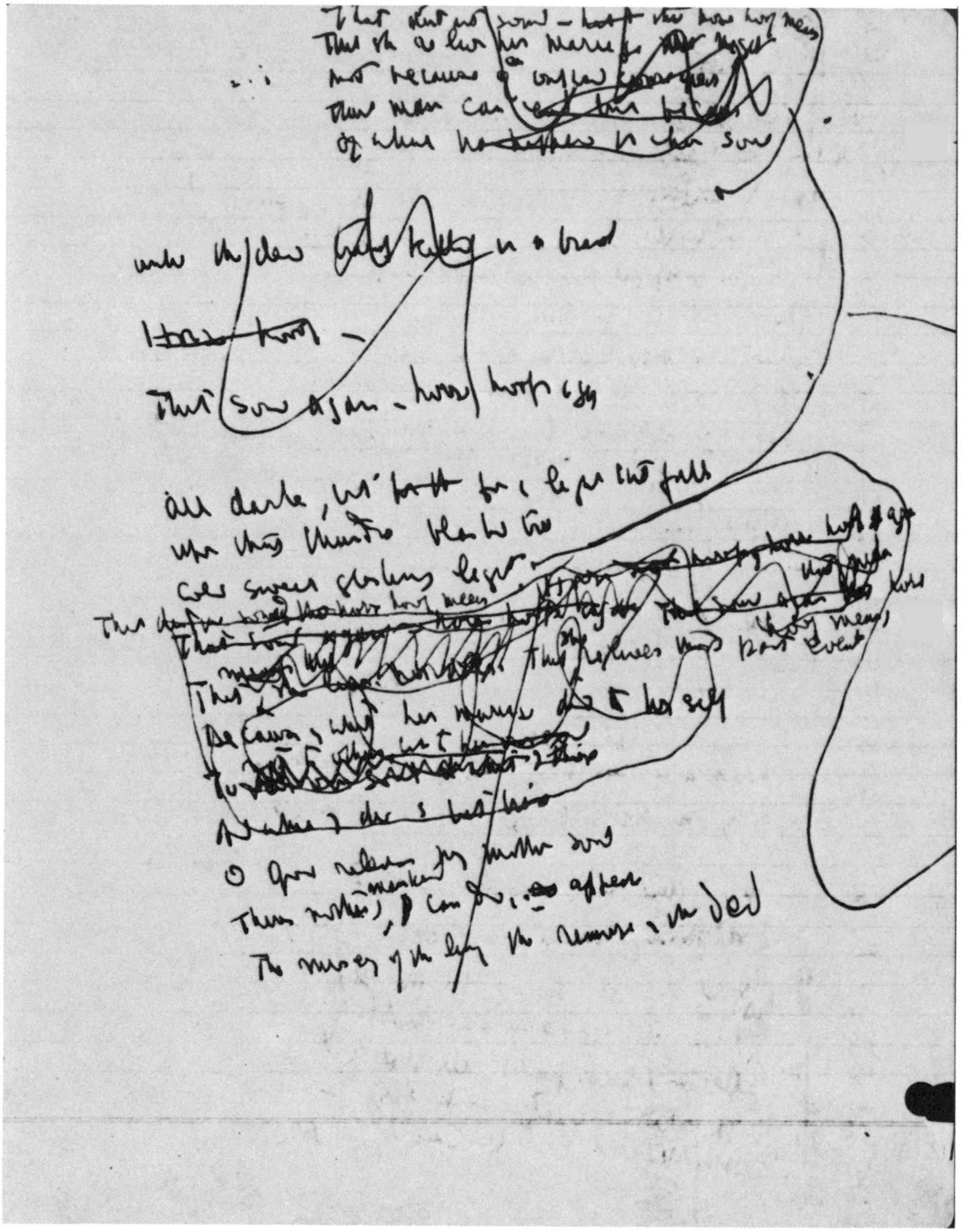

1 That distant sound— ~~hor [?]~~ that horse hoof means
2 That she relives her marriage ~~that~~ night
an
3 Not because of outward consequences
4 That man can end but because
5 Of what has happened in her soul
6 Until the dead tramp killed in a brawl
7 ~~Horse hoove~~ —
8 That sound again—horse hoofs again

9 All dark, but ~~for the~~ for [?] light that falls
10 Upon that thunder blasted tree
11 Cold sweet glistening light.
12 That distant sound that horse hoof means
13 ~~That sound again—horse hoofs again~~
means that
14 That∧she lives her deeds
15 Because of what her marriage did to her self
not to others but to her own soul
16 To ~~her own soul~~ & what I think
17 And what I did is but vain
18 O God release my mothers soul
mankind
19 There s nothing∧~~I~~ can do [?] appease
20 The misery of the living the remorse of the dead

---

a Horse ~~hoo~~ hoofs, horse hoofs ~~[?]~~ again
that means
b ~~That sound again the~~ horse
hoof means
she
c That∧relives that past event

1–5 These are revisions of ll. 12–17.
6–8 These lines were inscribed first as revisions of ll. 8–11, VA14r.
9–11 These were added but not retained on VA14r, although they were not cancelled.
12–17 The cancelled ll. 13–14 were revised in the right margin, and then both passages were entirely cancelled and further revised at the top of the page to become ll. 1–5.
a–b These are revisions of ll. 13–14.

13 ~~14~~

may
1 ~~And soon would take some woman s fancy~~
Old Man
~~outer~~ outer
2 He has come to the ~~front~~ room to find a glass
3 ~~A tired beast—where did I read these words~~
4 ~~Then the bride sleep fell upon Adam~~
5 He the tired beast wants a drink
This now he ~~& he~~
6 A tired beast now ~~he~~ wants a drink
7 This

This leaf, which is written in black ink, represents a stage of revision intermediary between VA12[r] and VA13[r] and VA14[r]. Probably Yeats wrote the number 14 in the upper right margin because l. 1 became VA14[r], l. 1; but he meant to write "13," to which he changed it.

1 This line is cancelled here but was retained on VA14[r], l. 1.

2–7 These lines were further revised on VA13[r], ll. 1–7, which supercede them.

and soon would take some woman's fancy IX
~~And [illegible] pass the blood [illegible] pollution~~ on
And so pass the pollution on
That I am a [illegible] for all men
~~And [illegible]~~ [illegible] ~~[illegible] the knife~~ in clean clean
In this hamlet ~~when this [illegible]~~ is clean
And I have picked up all ~~the~~ the dropt money
at [illegible] my [illegible]
I'll to a distant place ~~[illegible]~~ & steal
~~[illegible]~~ two
~~[illegible] the dead [illegible]~~ for nothing
what was the [illegible] for — for nothing
~~Dead [illegible]~~ and soon forgotten —

O God release my mother ~~[illegible]~~ for her use
For I can do no more ~~[illegible]~~ appease
The misery of the living the remorse of the dead

[illegible] [illegible], [illegible] [illegible],
~~[illegible]~~ — the [illegible] [illegible] men
That she must animate that dead night
Again & again ~~[illegible]~~ on, on, on, on
O God release my mother's soul
There nothing mankind can do appease
The misery of the living & the remorse of the dead

1 And soon would take some woman s fancy 14
2 ~~And he pass the blood polution~~ on
3 And so pass the polution on
{B
4 {but I am a wretched foul old man
when my
~~And so you~~ hate ~~my~~ the knife is ~~clea~~ clean
5 And there harmless ~~when this knife~~ is clean
all
6 And I have picked up ~~all~~ ~~the~~ dropped money
and change my trade
7 I ll to a distant place ~~[?and] there I [?tell]~~
8 ~~God listen & sing a song or~~ two
9 ~~About when the dead tramp killed for poluting~~
10 What was he killed for—poluting
11 Dead tramps are soon forgotten—
~~her past~~
from ~~her vision~~ the
12 O God release my mother ~~from her dream~~ from ~~her~~ vision
13 For I can do no more ~~le relea~~ appease
14 The misery of the living the remorse of the dead
15 Hoof beats, hoof beats,
hoof
16 ~~That distant sound~~—those ~~horse~~ beats mean
17 That she must animate that dead night
and
18 Again∧again ~~& again on—on~~ on, on, on, on
19 O God release my mother s soul
20 Theres nothing mankind can do appease
21 The misery of the living & the remorse of the dead

---

5 "there" appears to have a dot above "e" and may have been written as "their," although in either case the word is intended as "therefore."

1–11 After composing these lines Yeats cancelled ll. 8–11 and began to revise them on VA13v. Eventually he cancelled the revisions.

12–14 These were further revised on VA13v, ll. 18–20, and then revised yet again when they were transferred to this page to become ll. 19–21. In l. 12, possibly the inexplicable stroke attached to the letter "O" marks the beginning of a line that deletes "O God." Those words are treated here as having been inadvertently elided.

15–18 These were further revised as they were transferred from VA13v.

18 Either an ink blot or a comma appears after the second "again."

Manuscripts of the Second Verse Draft: *Souls in Purgatory*

MS 8771#3, which Yeats probably began early in April and completed before the end of the month, represents the second verse version of *Purgatory*. It is likely that he either dictated the first typescript from this manuscript or gave the manuscript to Mrs. Yeats, who then typed it herself. This is the only document among the published and unpublished materials in which he refers to the play as "Souls in Purgatory."

All of the leaves in MS 8771#3 represent revisions of leaves in MS 8771#2 except VB8^{v}, which is written in blue-green ink and with a distinctly wider nib than any used on other pages. Although the versos generally contain revisions of the rectos that follow them, VB8^{v} was filled before, rather than after, Yeats composed VB9^{r}. When he cancelled VB9^{r} he wrote "P.T.O." and then continued on VB9^{v} instead of the facing VB8^{v}, which he had already filled. The first line of VB8^{v}, "Begetting me," does appear on VB9^{r}, but little else suggests that the contents of VB8^{v} was incorporated into an earlier or a later draft. It is likely instead that the page represents a new direction that Yeats explored tentatively, but decided not to pursue, at some intermediary stage of composition. Lines 1–4, beginning with "Begetting me" and ending with "Come boy rack your wits," belong to the Old Man and so, too, do those that follow the ballad, but they are nowhere revised or incorporated into the manuscripts or typescripts. The three quatrains that follow are from F. R. Higgins's ballad "O Glory" (although Yeats has rearranged the order of the quatrains, omitted one of them entirely, ignored punctuation, and, presumably writing from memory, recorded the lines imperfectly).

Although the numbering of pages seems to suggest that there might have been an intermediary stage of revision, the leaves of which are lost, it seems more likely that in composing Yeats proceeded as far as page 7^{r}. He then decided to rewrite a new page 7, the current one, only half of which is filled. The page that continues the text from where the revised page 7 leaves off was originally numbered 11. Since this page does continue the text from page 7, it seems likely that after having reworked page 7, Yeats, when he was ready to go on, accidentally numbered the four following pages 11, 12, 13, 14. Then, he renumbered page 11 as 8, page 12 as 9, page 13 as 10, and page 14 as 11. In turn, when revising page 9 or its verso, he used the number 9a; he then changed 9a to 10 and added the leaf 10a. The use of 10 and 10a meant that the page numbered 13 and then 10 had to be changed to 11; and the page numbered 14 and then 11 had to be changed to 12.

There is, in addition, one unpaginated recto leaf written in black ink which represents lines that are intermediary between VB11^{r} and VB12^{r}. The seven lines on this page, which is designated VB11i^{r}, were further revised on VB12^{r}.

Scene in Purgatory 1

a ruined house & a bare tree in the back ground. moon light

Boy

Half door, hall door, ~~front door, back door~~
Hither & thither, ~~[illegible]~~ day & night.
~~And here [illegible]~~
Holding up this old pack ~~upon my shoulder~~
Hearing your talk

Old Man

I think about that study ~~this~~ house
~~my thought [illegible]~~ on its jokes & stories
I try to remember what the butler
Said to a drunken game keeper
In mid October but I cannot
I cannot & none living can
Where are the jokes & stories of a house
Its threshold gone to patch a pig stye

Boy

What do you know about this place?

Old Man

The moon light falls upon the path
The shadow of a cloud upon the house
And that is symbolical; study that tree
What is it like.

Boy

A silly old man

Old Man

Its like — no matter what its like
I saw it a year ago stripped bare as now
~~[illegible] fifty years ago I saw that tree~~ I saw it fifty years ago

Souls in Purgatory 1

a ruined house & a bare tree in the back ground. Moon light

Boy

1 Half door, hall door, ~~front door, back door~~
Hither & thither, ~~hill &~~ day & night
2 ~~And here no door at all & all the while~~
up this old
3 Holding ~~this~~^pack ~~upon my shoulder~~
4 Hearing you talk

Old Man

that
I think about study ~~this~~ house
5 ~~My thoughts are on~~ its jokes & stories
6 I try to remember what the butler
7 Said to a drunken game keeper
8 In mid October but I cannot
none
9 I cannot & ~~nob~~ living can
10 Where are the jokes & stories of a house
11 Its threshold gone to patch a pigstie

Boy

12 What do you know about this place?

Old Man

13 The moon light falls upon the path
14 The shadow of a cloud upon the house
that
15 And that s symbolical; study ~~th~~ tree
16 What is it like.

Boy

17 ~~Boy~~ a silly old man

Old Man A ~~silly old man~~

19 Its like—no matter what its like
20 I saw it a year ago stripped bare as now
21 ~~But fifty years ago I saw that tree~~ I saw it fifty years ago

---

5 Probably a comma after "on"; possibly an ink blot.

2

Before the thunder bolt had riven it
Green leaves, ripe leaves, leaves thick as butter
Fat greasy life. Stand ~~[illegible]~~ there & look
~~[illegible]~~ Because there is somebody in ~~the~~ [above: that] house
The boy puts down pack & stands in the doorway

Boy

There's nobody ~~[illegible]~~ here

Old Man

There's somebody in that house

Boy

The floor is gone; the windows gone
And where there should be roof there's sky
And here's a bit of an egg shell thrown
Out of a jackdaw's nest

Old Man

But there are some
That do not care what's gone, what's left,
The souls in purgatory [above: that] come back
To habitations & familiar spots

Boy

Your wits are out again.

Old Man

~~[illegible]~~ Relive
~~[illegible]~~ Transgression & that not once
~~[illegible]~~ But many times; they know at last
~~Again & again — They [illegible]~~
The consequence of that transgression

2

1 Before the thunder bolt had riven it
2 Green leaves, ripe leaves, leaves thick as butter
3 Fat greasy life. Stand in ~~that door~~ there & look
{B that
4 ~~Look~~ {because there somebody in ~~the~~ house
The boy puts down pack & stands in the door way

Boy

5 There s nobody ~~in the~~ here

Old Man

6 Theres some body in that house

Boy

7 The floor is gone; the windows gone
8 And where there should be roof there s sky
9 And here a bit of an egg shell thrown
10 Out of a jackdaws nest

Old Man

11 But there are some
12 That do not care what s gone, whats left,
that
13 The souls in purgatory^come back
14 To habitations & familiar spots

Boy

15 Your wits are out again

Old Man

16 ~~The lives~~ Relive
17 ~~Through all transgressions of their lives~~ Transgressions & that not once
~~Not once but many times~~
18 ~~Again & again~~ — ~~They know at last~~ But many times & they know at last
19 The consequences of those transgressions

---

3 Possibly a dash before "door."
4 "there" possibly "theres."
9 "here" possibly "heres."
16 Possibly "Their" or "There" before "lives."

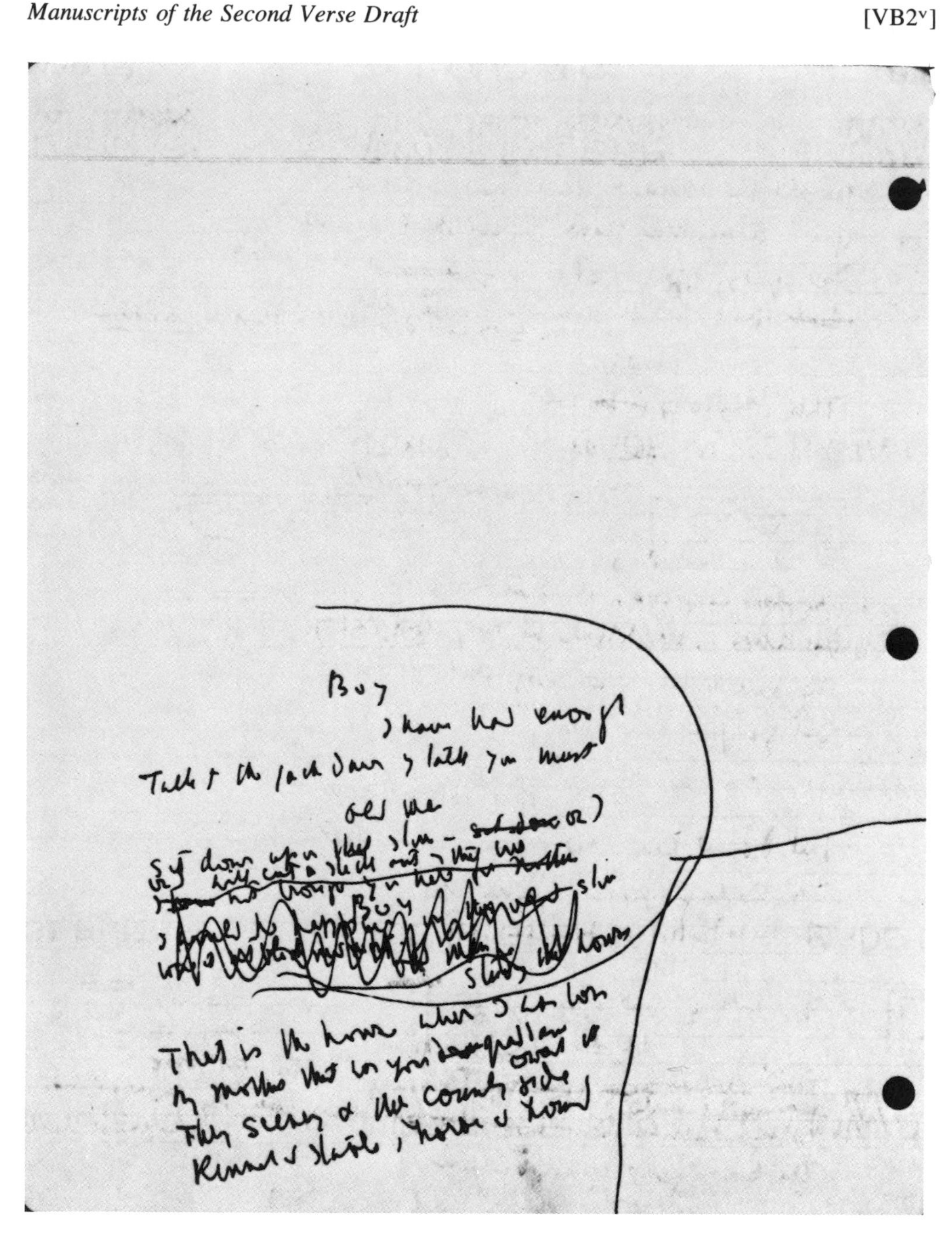

Boy
I have had enough
Talk to the jackdaw if talk you must
Old Man
Sit down upon that stone
That is the house where I was born
My mother that was your grand dam owned it
This scenery & the country side
Kennel & stable, horse & hound

Boy

1 I have had enough
2 Talk to the jack daws if talk you must

Old Man

3 Sit down upon this stone— ~~sit down~~ or I
4 Or I will cut a stick out of that tree
5 ~~I have not brought you here for nothing~~

Boy

6 I would be happier on this old stone
7 Were it not black midnight

Old Man

8 Study that house
9 That is the house where I was born
10 My mother that was your ~~[?]~~ granddam owned it
11 This scenery & the country side
12 Kennel & stable, horse & hound

The directional lines connect with VB3^{r}.

1–12 These were composed later than VB3^{r}, ll. 1–24. Lines 1–5 are revisions of VB3^{r}, ll. 19–24. Lines 1–8 were not retained, but the new lines (9–12), were.

3

1 And here s a bit of an egg shell thrown
nest or a jack daws nest \
2 Out of a stares ~~or jack daws nest~~
Old Man
3 Theres somebody in that house: a year ago
4 I stood where now I stand, & I saw
5 The souls of purgatory in that house
6 First one & then another came
7 And stood in the window. There in it yet
8 All souls in purgatory come back
habitations
9 To ~~habitations~~ & familiar spots
10 And there live through their old transgressions
yet
11 Again & again. They know at last
12 ~~The [?] every consequence of those transgressions~~
13 Whether upon others or upon them selves
14 If upon others others may bring help
15 For when the consequences ~~end~~ is at an end
16 The dream must end; if upon them selves
17 These is no help but in themselves
18 And in God s mercy
Boy
19 ~~The books you read~~ I have had enough
20 In grandad s library put you astray.
21 ~~In [?]~~
~~Old Man~~
22 But ~~I have enough good~~ by
23 Talk ~~to the jack daws~~
Old Man (Threatening him with the stick.)
24 Sit down. Sit down.

---

a The souls in purgatory are there

b But there are some
whats left
c That do not care what s gone/

---

a This line is a revision of l. 5.
b–c These lines were revised on VB2v, ll. 1–4.

Old Man

1 ~~This is the house where~~ I was born

2 This is the house where I was born
Boy
I would be happier on this old stone
3 ~~I d take more interest in these old stones~~
Were it not black night
4 ~~Were not midnight~~.
Old Man
5 ~~She had riches~~ Your grand dam boy
6 ~~She had horses, she had stables she had~~ horses
owned
7 My mother ~~own~~ the house, owned all
8 This scenery & the country side
[?]
9 ~~[? ?∧?] horses, every~~ thing
10 Kennel & stable, horse & hound

ed
11 Look∧at him & married him
every thing
12 And he squandered ~~all that~~ she had
13 She never knew the worst, ~~of it~~ because
she died in
14 ~~Because~~ ~~she~~ ~~die in~~ giving birth to me
s
15 But now she kno∧it all being dead

The directional lines connect with VB4^{r}.

1–4 After Yeats cancelled l. 1, he reproduced the cancelled line as part of a longer passage that was to replace ll. 8–9, VB4^{r}; he then added ll. 3–4.

5–10 These lines are revisions of VB4^{r}, ll. 10–14, which were cancelled before these were.

11–15 These are new lines to follow l. 21, VB4^{r}.

13 The comma after ''worst'' was probably inserted after ''of it'' was cancelled.

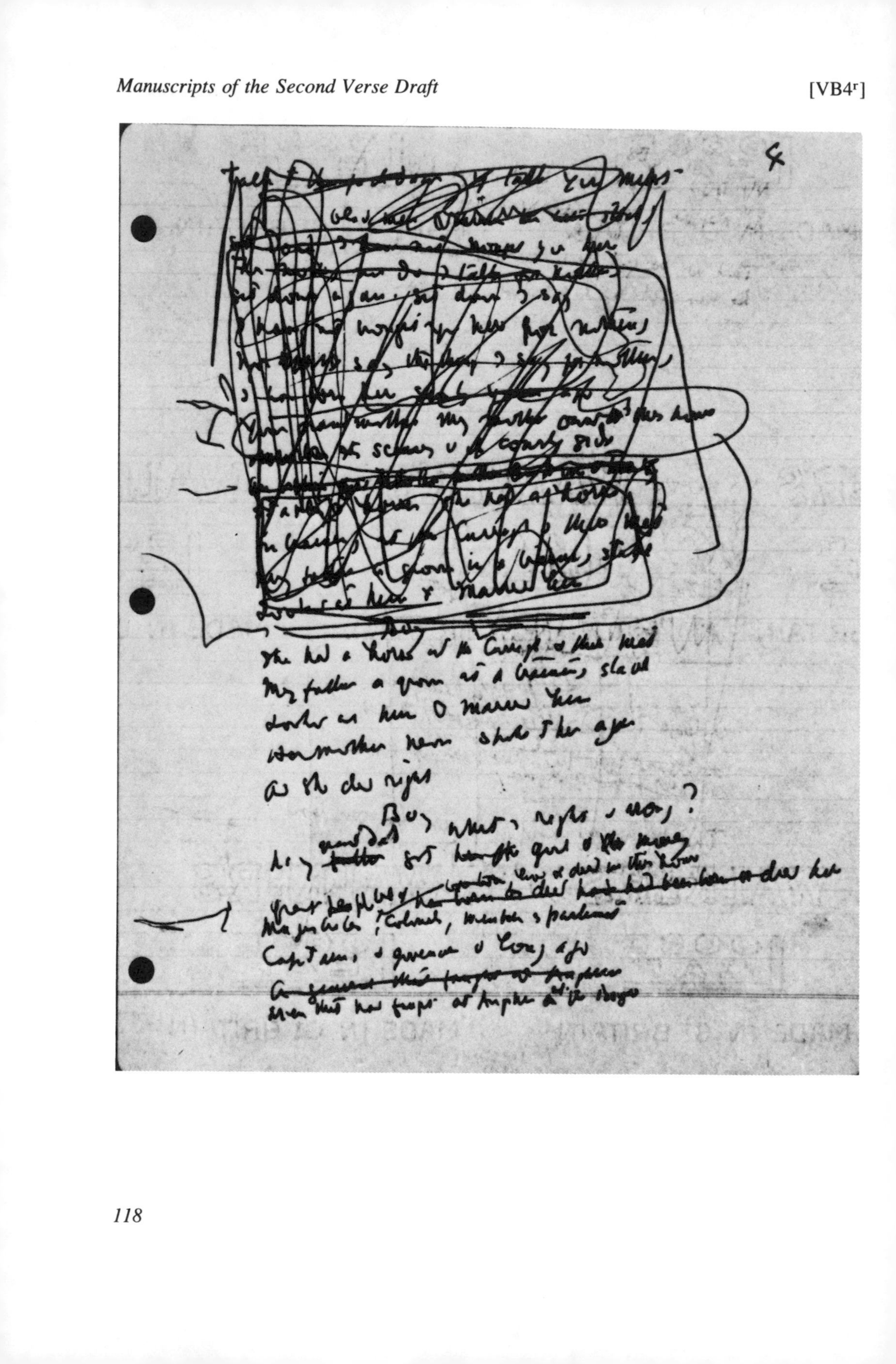

4

1 Talk to the jackdaws if talk you must

Old Man (threatening him with stick)

2 Sit down I have not brought you here
3 For nothing nor do I talk for nothing
4 Sit down again. Sit down I say
5 I have not brought you here for nothing
6 Nor ~~[?]~~ say the things I say for nothing
7 I was born here sixty years ago
8 Your grand mother my mother owned [?] this house
9 ~~Its trees~~ Its scenery & its country side
10 ~~An orphan girl~~ ~~Fatherless motherless & one & twenty~~
11 Stables & horses She had a horse
12 In training at the Curragh & there met
13 My father a groom in a training stable
14 Looked at him & married him

Boy

15 She had a house at the Curragh & there met
16 My father a groom at a training stable
17 Looked at him & married him
18 Her mother never spoke to her again
19 And she did right

Boy

20 What s right & wrong?

grand dad

21 My ~~father~~ got ~~her~~ ~~the~~ girl & ~~the~~ money

~~were born,~~ lived & died in this house

22 Great people were^ ~~ha born or died~~ ~~had had been born or died~~ here
23 Magistrates, colonels, members of parliament
24 Captains & governors & long ago
25 ~~A general that fought at Aughrim~~

at

26 Men that have fought at Aughrim & the Boyne

The directional lines connect with those on VB3^{v}.

8–9 These were revised on VB3^{v}, ll. 1–4. Possibly one or more cancelled letters after "owned."

10–14 These were revised on VB3^{v}, ll. 5–10.

21 Lines 11–15, VB3^{v}, were to follow this line.

22 The caret after "people" points to "were born" above "born."

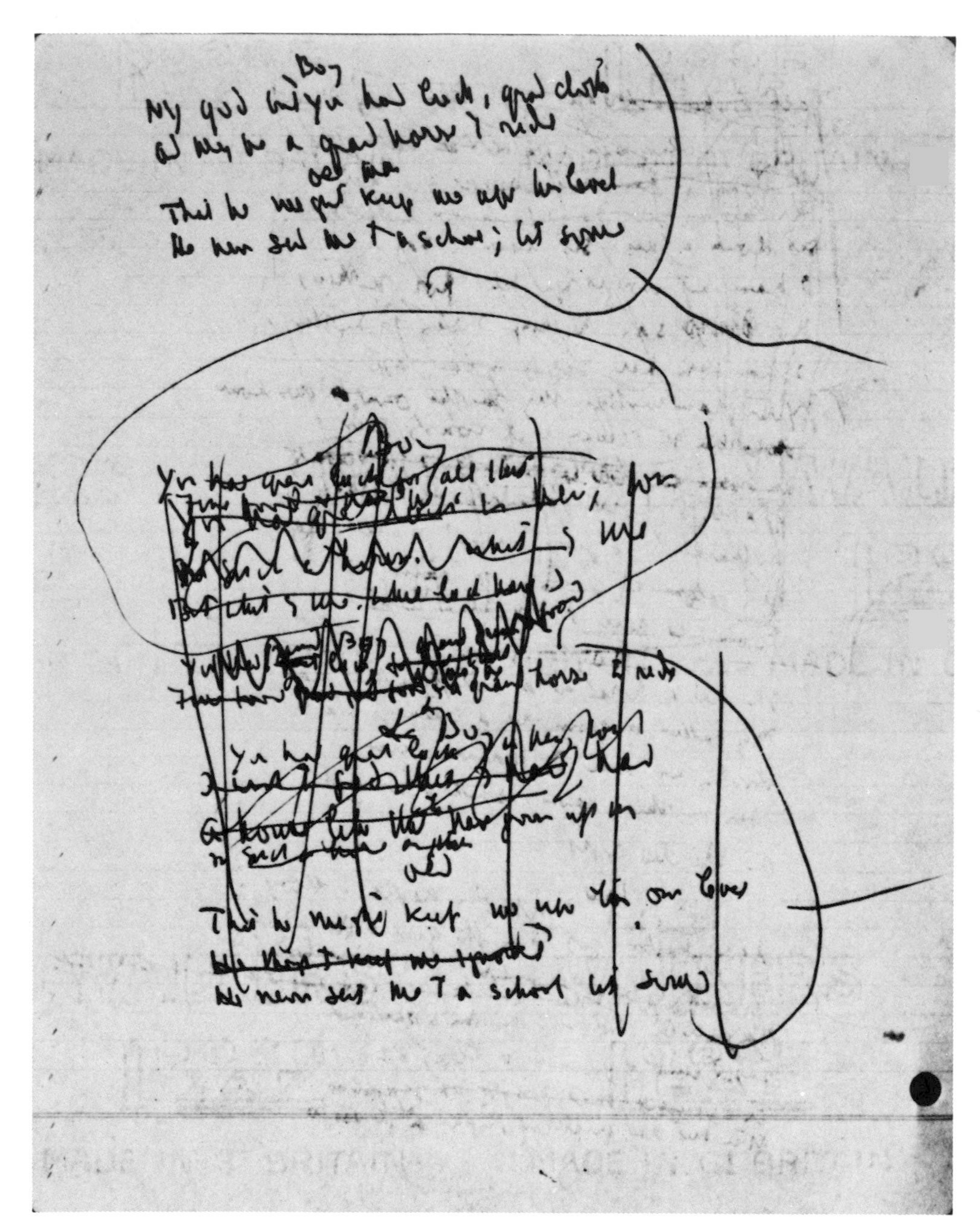

Boy
My god but you had luck, good clothes
And may be a good horse to ride
That he might keep me upon his level
He never sent me to a school; but some

That he might keep me upon the one level
He never sent me to a school but some

Boy
1 My god but you had luck, grand clothes
2 And may be a grand horse to ride
Old Man
3 That he might keep me upon his level
4 He never sent me to a school; but some

Boy
5 You had great luck for all that
Fine food & wine
6 ~~You had great luck in being~~ born
7 ~~In such a house. What~~ of me
8 ~~But what of me. What luck have~~ I
grand Boy grand drink & food
9 You had ~~great~~ luck, ~~for all that~~
and may be
10 ~~Fine food~~ ~~grand [?] food~~∧& a grand horse to ride
Boy
11 You had great luck in being born
12 ~~I wish to god that I had~~ had
to
13 ~~A house like that∧have grown~~ up in
14 In ~~such a house~~ ~~as this~~
Old
15 That he might keep me upon his own level
16 ~~He thought to keep me ignorant~~
17 He never sent me to a school but some

1–4 These are further revisions of ll. 11–17, VB4v, which were cancelled and further revised as ll. 5–10, VB4v.
10 The illegible word is possibly "wine." Possibly a caret to the left of "Boy" after l. 10.
13 The caret has been moved from the line below.

5

Had loved the house had loved all
Something had gone on forever [illegible]
To dance at [illegible] can hear it die
Or [illegible] in every sphere
To [illegible] the things blossom in the past
They had loved the trees that he cut down
To pay what he had lost at cards
Or spent on horses, [illegible] drink & women
[illegible] The inherited [illegible] the house
But he [illegible] the house; to [illegible] a house
Where great men grew up, married & died
I have declared a competition [illegible]

[illegible]

Half loves me for my half of [illegible].
A [illegible]: half laughs at [illegible]
A Catholic [illegible] laugh at [illegible]
There are old books & tales made fine
By [illegible] [illegible] [illegible], books
Modern & ancient, [illegible] books of the [illegible]

1 Had loved the house had loved all 5
2 Some that had gone on government work
3 To London or to India came home to die
4 Or ~~sp~~ came from London every spring
~~see~~ look at
5 To ~~look at~~ the May blossom in the park
6 They had loved the trees that he cut down
7 To pay what he had lost at cards
8 Or spent on horses, ~~& on women~~ drink & women
{T
9 ~~Had loved~~ {the intricate passages of the house
~~murdered~~ ~~murder~~
10stet But he ~~killed~~ the house; to kill a house
11 Where great men grew up, married, ~~died~~ died
~~[?is]~~
12 I here declare∧a capital offence
scarcely knew it
13 ~~My mother never knew the worst~~
14 She died in giving my ~~mother died in giving~~ birth to me
15 My mother schar knew a quarter of the tale
16 ~~My mother saw it all begin~~
My ~~di~~ mother
17 But∧died in giving birth to me
at the
therefore , it all
And ~~that~~ did not know ~~because~~
18 ~~But now knows all~~ be But now she must know every thing,
19 But now knows everything because
20 A soul in Purgatory knows everything.
21 When I grew up Here I grew up & here my father
upon
22 That he might keep me ~~on~~ his own level
23 Refused me education but ~~some~~ some
24 Half loved me for my half of her.
25 A game keeper s wife taught me to read
26 A Catholic curate taught me Latin
& books
27 There were old books∧made fine
28 By eighteenth century French bindings, books
29 Modern & ancient, ~~a ton of books~~ books by the ton

Directional lines connect with VB4v.

1 This line continues the revision of l. 9: Yeats neglected to cancel "Had loved the house"; "had loved all" was to replace "Had loved," l. 9, but he also neglected to adjust the upper- and lowercase letters.

10 "killed" below "murdered," both of which were underscored and the word "stet" written in the left margin.

13–20 These were neither revised on VB4v nor retained.

15 It is possible that Yeats began to write "scarcely," decided to write "hardly," and actually wrote neither one.

24–29 These continue from l. 4, VB4v.

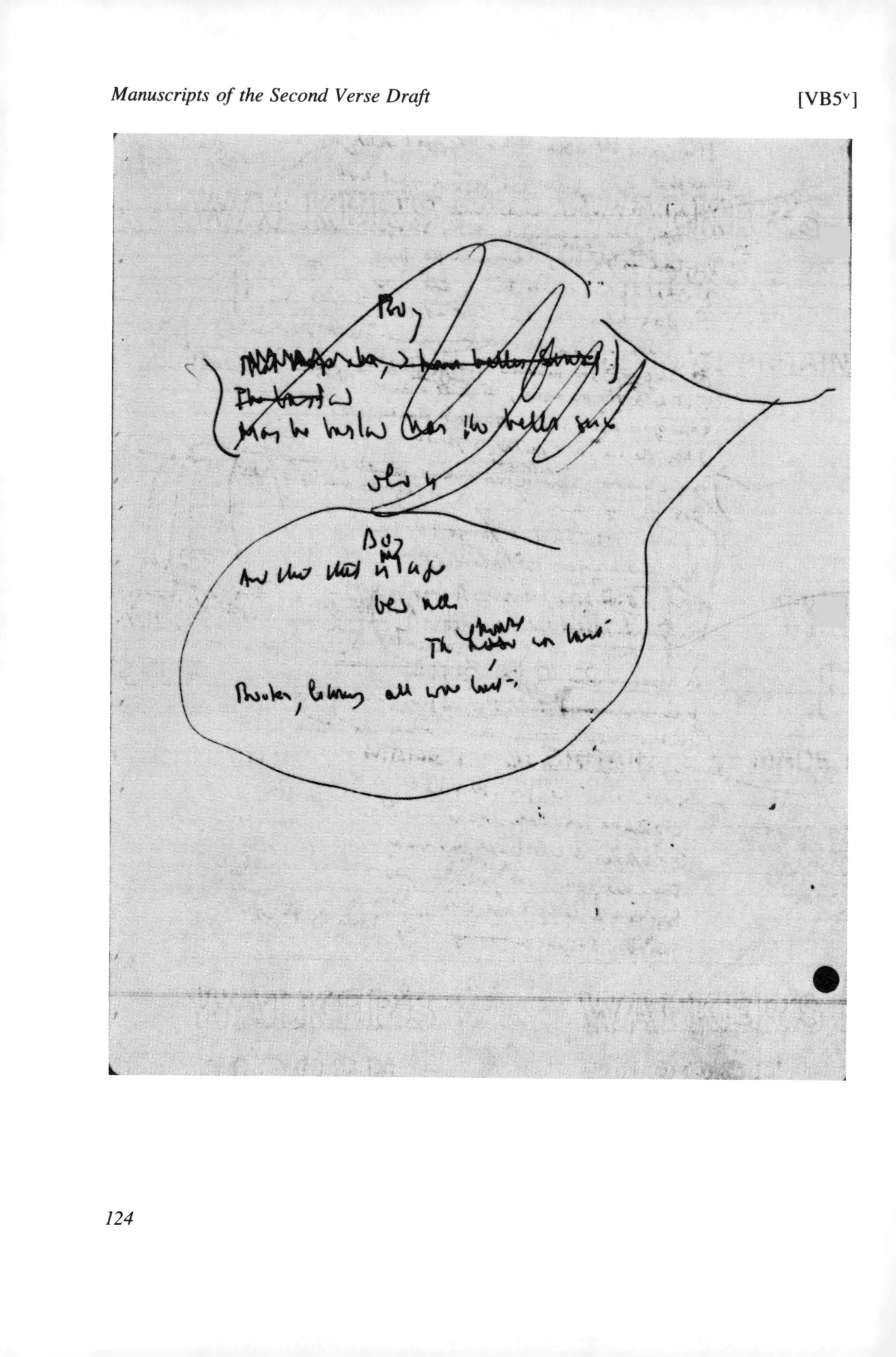

Boy
1 ~~That [?] be, I have better sense~~
2 ~~The bastard~~
3 May be bastard has the better sense
Old M
Boy
my
4 And that that is age
Old Man
house
5 The ~~house~~ was burnt
6 Books, library all were burnt.

The directional lines connect with VB6r.
1–6 Line 3 was retained to follow l. 4, VB6r, but was then cancelled and further revised as ll. 4–6 of VB5v.

6

Boy

What education ~~have you given~~ have you given me

Old man

I gave the education that befits
A [illegible] a peddler [illegible] got
Upon a tinker's daughter in a ditch.
When I had reached my [illegible] year fifteen year
~~The house is burnt & all was burned~~
My father set it on fire when drunk

Boy

And is it true what people say
That you killed him in the burning house

Old man

I have never [illegible] on his [illegible]

Boy

Nobody father — I stuck him with a knife
~~[illegible]~~
~~[illegible]~~ That knife [illegible]
~~[illegible]~~
~~And after that I dragged him to the fire~~
And after that I dragged him to the fire
Then dragged him out Somebody saw
The knife thrown ~~[illegible]~~ could not be certain
Because the body was all black & charred
Then some that were his drunken friends
Swore that they would put me upon trial
~~[illegible]~~ spoke of quarrels & a threat
~~And then~~ some that I [illegible] gave me some old clothes
I [illegible] — ~~[illegible]~~ worked here & there
Until I became a peddler on the road

6

Boy
1 What education ~~have you given me~~ have you given me
Old Man
2 I gave the education that befits
~~bas~~ bastard got
3 A ~~lad begotten~~ by a pedlar ~~father~~ got
4 Upon a tinkers daughter in a ditch.
~~seventeenth~~
5 When I had reached my ~~eighteenth~~∧year fifteenth year
6 ~~The house its books & all were burnt~~
7 My father set it upon fire when drunk
Boy
8 And is it true what people say
9 That you killed him in the burning house
Old Man
here,
10 ~~Is~~ there nobody∧but our two selves
Boy
Old Man
11 Nobody father— stuck him
I ~~drove~~ a knife
dinner
12 ~~Between his third & second rib~~ ~~That old jack knife that cuts my~~∧
13 ~~Then dragged him out & made~~ belief That knife that cuts my ~~d d~~ dinner now
14 [~~That I had saved him from the fire~~
15 [~~And after that I draged him from the fire~~
16 And after that I dropped him in the fire
him
17 Then dragged∧out some body ~~sai~~ saw
wound
18 The knife∧~~wound~~ but ~~he was not sure~~ could not be certain
19 Because the body was all black & charred
Then
20 ~~But~~ some that were his drunken friends
21 Swore that they would put me upon trial
22 ~~There had been threats & quarrels between us~~ spoke of quarrels & of threats
~~The~~ But the
23 ~~But~~ ~~The~~∧game keeper gave me some old clothes
ran away
24 I ~~fled~~ — ~~did odd jobs here & there~~ worked here & there
25 Until I became a pedlar on the roads

The directional lines connect with VB5^v.
10 "there" probably intended as "There's."

7

no good bride but good enough
Because I am my fathers son
Because of what I did you may do

~~[illegible]~~

~~[illegible]~~
Listen to the hoof beats—listen listen
~~This night is the anniversary~~
~~Of my mothers wedding night~~
~~The night wherein I was begot~~

Boy

I cannot hear a sound

Old Man

Beat. Beat.

This night is the anniversary
Of my mothers wedding night
Or of the night wherein I was begot

1 No good trade but good enough 7
2 Because I am my father s son
3 Because of what I did & yet may do
4 ~~This is the knife blade—fifty years, fifty years~~
5 ~~But listen. Listen. Beat. Beat.~~
6 Listen to the hoof beats—listen listen
7 This night is the aniversary
8 Of my mothers [?] wedding night
9 ~~The night where in I was begot~~

Boy

10 I cannot hear a sound

Old Man

Beat. Beat.

11 This night is the aniversary
12 Of my mothers wedding night
13 Or of the night wherein I was begot

This page was probably prepared from an earlier version contained on one or more discarded leaves.
8 ''mothers'' possibly followed by one or more cancelled letters.

1 O do not let him touch you. It is not true
2 That drunken men cannot beget
3 And if he touch he must beget
4 And you must bare his murderer
5 Deaf, both deaf; if I should throw
6 A stick or a stone they would not hear
7 And that s a proof my wits are out
8 ~~B~~

L

The inverted "7" that appears in the lower left quarter of this leaf was probably inscribed by mistake. When Yeats discovered the double-ruled bar was at the top instead of at the bottom, as it is on all of the other leaves of *Purgatory,* rather than turn the page round, in which case the holes would have been on the wrong side for a recto page, he turned and flipped the leaf, wrote the number "7" again, and composed the new page 7. But he neglected to cancel the number "7" on the verso side.

The directional line connects with VB8r.

1–8 These lines were added to follow l. 26, VB8r.

4 "bare" intended as "bear."

45

Old man

My father is riding from the public house

A whiskey bottle under his arm

Look at the window — she stands there

[illegible] the servants are all in bed

She is alone; he has stayed late

Bragging & drinking in the public house

Boy

There nothing in the window; all there is black

You have made it up. You you are mad

You are getting madder every day

Old man

The hoof beats [illegible] now it beats

[illegible] gravelled avenue

[illegible] grass grown now — the hoof beat stops

He has gone to the other side of the house

To put the horse up — all that is hidden

But I can see it all in the mind

She has gone down & open the door

This night she is no better than her man

~~He is half drunk [illegible]~~

And does not mind that he is half drunk

Because she is mad about him. They mount

She leads him into her own chamber

For that is the marriage chamber now

The window is dimly lit again

Because she has put the candle on the table

And the passage door is open — now

[illegible] the door is shut and the window dark

(The window is lit [illegible] showing a young girl [illegible])

~~Old Man~~ ~~11~~ 8

1 My father is riding from the public house
2 A whiskey bottle under his arm

showing a young girl).
(The window is lit ~~up, a girl~~ stands ~~there~~)

3 Look at the window—she stands there
4 Listening; the servants are all in bed
5 She is alone; he has stayed late
6 Bragging & drinking in the public house

Boy

7 Theres nothing in the window; all there is black;
8 You have made it up. Now you are mad
You
9 ^And getting madder every day

Old Man

10 The hoof beats louder now it beats
11 Upon a gravelled avenue
12 Where grass grows now—The hoof beat stops
13 He has gone to the other side of the house
14 To put the horse up—all that is hidden
15 But I can see it all in the mind
16 She has gone down to open the door
17 This night she is no better than her man
18 ~~He is half drunk but she is mad about him~~
19 And does not mind that he is half drunk
20 Because she is mad about him. They mount
21 She brings him into her own chamber
22 For that is the marriage chamber now
23 The window is dimly lit again
24 Because she has put the candle on the table
25 And the passage door is open—now
26 ~~Because~~ that door is shut and the window dark

The directional lines connect with VB7v.

The number "11" was probably inscribed by mistake after having prepared the new page 7 from one or more pages that were possibly too heavily revised and therefore discarded. Eventually he corrected the pagination by cancelling "11" and replacing it with "8."

1 Begetting me.
verse a good bawdy
2 Lift up a ~~good bawdy song~~ verse
do
3 Any thing will ~~do~~^if its merry enough
4 Come boy come rack your wits

5 To blazes with gold the high king of all metals
6 With soft talk & kisses well never lack victuals
7 And the [?] west of a ditch is best ~~mat~~ settles
8 Glory O glory O when the evening de clines

9 Before the black hunger I d husbands in plenty
10 And may be your grand dad was one of the many
11 Now was he this red coat he better than any
12 Glory O glory how swigged down the wine

13 O [?] young for my age & I dont need a wattle
not dry as a nettle
14 O I am young for my age & ~~I dont ne~~
15 So you clout the pot & I ll clout the kettle
16 Glory O glory O so well both keep in time
that song grand mother
17 But she that sang was old & ~~my mother~~ was
18 ~~Young—four & twenty I dare say—but she~~
19 ~~Could~~ clout ~~the kettle~~
20 And your mother boy was but four & twenty
21 And doubtless boy she had the trick of it
22 And could clout the kettle

This page is written in blue-green ink and was filled before rather than after VB9^{r}.

1–4 It is likely these lines, which belong to the Old Man, represent a new direction Yeats explored but decided not to pursue. In l. 2, "song" was cancelled before the entire line was cancelled.

5–12 These are three of four quatrains Yeats recorded imperfectly and in an order that differs from the printed version in *A Broadside* (no. 7, new series, July 1937) of the ballad "O Glory" by F. R. Higgins. In l. 7, there is either one cancelled letter or an ink blot after "the"; probably "the" omitted after "is"; "of all" omitted after "best"; and, "he" omitted after "how" in l. 12.

13 The indecipherable word is probably "I'm."

17–22 These lines, which belong to the Boy, are adapted to the dramatic context of *Purgatory* from the first quatrain of "O Glory."

17 "grand mother" is possibly cancelled.

But
1 And here s a problem ~~boy~~—she must live ~~12~~ 9
2 Through every thing in exact detail
3 Driven to it by remorse & yet
4 Can she renew the sexual act
5 And find no pleasure in it & if not
6 If pleasure & remorse must both be there
7 Which is the greater—I lack schooling
8 Go fetch Turtullian; he & I
9 Will ravel all that problem out
10 ~~While a couple couple~~ that ~~pair lie~~ begetting
11 ~~While that couple upon~~
12 While those two lie upon the matress
13 Begetting me.
14 Come back, come back come back I say
15 ~~Come back & show me what you have got~~
16 ~~You thought I could not talk & see~~
might rob me while I talk
17 You thought ~~that you could rob me whi~~
18 Imagining I could talk & see
You
19 You ~~And~~ rumaged in the pack—Robbed by them both
20 Robbed by father robbed by son
21 And may be it ~~it~~ s but natural
22 That beast rob beast
23 Show what you have got
Boy
24 You kept it all—never gave me a share
25 I will keep it all—you ~~killing~~ killed my grand dad
26 Because you were young & he was old
27 But now I am young & you are old
28 And if you touch me I will strangle you.
(They struggle—the [?] boy dropping money onto the stage)
29 O my god—there, ~~there~~ in the window
30 He was not telling lies at all
31 The upper window is lit up

P.T.O.

The number "12," in the upper right margin, which was written by mistake, was cancelled and then replaced with the number "9."

7 Possibly a period rather than a dash after "greater."

13 It may have been when Yeats actually reached this line or, more likely, imagined having reached this line, that he explored the possibility of adding ll. 1–4 and the ballad that follows on VB8v.

14–31 When Yeats reached l. 31 and found the verso of VB8 filled, he wrote "P.T.O" and revised these lines on the verso of VB9.

~~9a~~ 10

1 Come back, come back
2 ~~Where are you going & So that~~ is it
3 And so you thought to slink away
4 My bag of money in your fingers
5 And that I could not talk & see
6 You have been rumaging in the pack
has
(The light in the window^faded out)
Boy
7 You kept it all & never gave me a share
Old Man
8 And had I given it young as you are
9 You would have spent it upon drink
Boy
10 What if I did. I have a right
as I like
11 To get my share & spend it ~~upon~~^
Old Man
12 Give me that bag & no more words
Boy
13 What if I kill you—you killed grandad
14 Because you were young & he was old
15 Now I am young & you are old
down
{d
~~takes the bag~~. knocks the lad {out
(~~They struggle.~~ The Old Man ~~throws the lad~~ ~~down~~
16 The pack falls and the money rolls out)
Old Man
Get up & of
17 ~~Get up & [?]~~ pick up that money. ~~Some^it is over there~~
Boy (beginning to pick up money mutters)
18 Knocked about—ordered about—no luck
19 O my god. There is the window all lit up
20 He was not telling lies at all
21 ~~The window s all lit All lit up just as he said~~

This page is a revision of VB9r, ll. 14–31.
11 The caret after "upon" is possibly a dash.
Directions after l. 15: the period after "struggle" is possibly a dash; "d" is possibly cancelled and "out" is written over it.
16 "and" is possibly cancelled.

Boy (picking up money) 10a

1 Knocked about; ordered about

a man is pouring whiskey into a glass

(The window is lit up & man ~~st leans against the wall glass in~~ hand

2 My god the window is lit up

3 And somebody stands there; although

are all

4 The floor boards ~~have been~~ burned away

When Yeats reached the bottom of VB9^v, he continued on the recto of the leaf he paginated as 10a.

1 ~~All light~~ has
2 The stage has grown dim, except where
3 the tree stands in white light

4 and I lack rhyme
∧
the
5 ~~A~~ Study ~~that~~ tree
6 That stands there like a purified soul
c
7 All {sold sweet glistening light
is
8 Dear mother the window dark again
9 But you are in the light because
10 I finished all that consequence

The directional line connects with VB11^{r}. Lines 1–3, which represent stage directions, were probably added after Yeats composed ll. 5–10.

1–7 These are revisions of VB11^{r}, ll. 20–22, which revisions were probably added after ll. 23–27 were written. The passage was further revised and was to follow VB11^{r}, l. 19.

[illegible] 11

old me [illegible] because my father

The wonder [illegible] [illegible] [illegible]

[illegible] He has come [illegible] & find a place for [illegible] He came, then [illegible] into some tired heart

Then the wonder sleep fell upon Adam

When did I read [illegible] and yet

There is nothing s[illegible] in the wonder then

But the professor upon my mother's mind

Being dead she is

alone in her memory

That [illegible] would know nothing being nothing

If I should kill a man under the wonder the wonder goes dark

He would not even turn his head. (He stabs boy).

My father and my son and the same jack knife

That finishes [illegible] – there – there – there

(He [illegible]) ([illegible] a [illegible],

Hush a by [illegible] boy, Thy father's a knight

Thy mother a lady, lovely and bright,

No that is somewhere, that I read in a book

And if I sing, it must be to my mother

And [illegible] Dear mother

Because [illegible] all this evil

The wonder [illegible] but peace

I killed that lad because had he grown

He would soon take some woman's fancy

Beget and pass pollution on

I am a wretched foul old man [illegible]

And therefore [illegible] harmless – [illegible]

what I have [illegible]

Old Man

is lit because my father ~~13~~ ~~10~~ 11

1 The window ~~has~~ ~~lighted~~^ ~~up because~~ the
2 He has come all lit up
3 The window is ~~lighted up because~~
in
4 ~~He come for a glass into the front room~~
5 ~~A tired beast & he wants her dream,~~
6 Then the bride sleep fell upon Adam
7 Where did I read those words & yet
leaning
8 There is nothing ~~standing~~ in the window there
9 But the impression upon my mothers mind
Being dead she is
10 ~~She is~~^alone in her remorse
That beast ~~He~~ there
11 ~~That beast there~~ would know nothing being nothing
12 If I should kill a man under the window
The window goes dark
13 He would not even turn his head. (He stabs boy.
son and the same jack knife
14 My father & my ~~son son on the j~~
15 ~~There—there—~~ That finishes ~~ther~~—there—there—there
(He stabs again & again & then sings) (~~He [?] stabs again~~ & again)
16 Hush a by ~~bod~~ bady Thy father s a knight
17 Thy mothers a lady lovely & bright.
18 No that is something that I read in a book
19 And if I sing it ~~my~~ must be to my mother
20 And ~~I have not the words—Dear mother~~
21 ~~Because I have~~ finished all that evil
22 The windows dark again Sink into peace
23 I killed that lad because of his youth
24 He would soon take some ~~fa~~ woman s fancy
25 Beget & pass polution on
26 I am a wretched foul old man
~~that I have~~ stuck
27 And there ~~fore~~ there for harm less— ~~The knife now I stick~~
When I have stuck

---

a Has come ~~into the front room for a glass~~
to find a glass for his whiskey
b He leans there ~~now~~ ~~like~~ looks
c like some tired beast

Yeats adjusted the pagination after cancelling "13" and "10" in the upper right margin.
1 Yeats probably intended to cancel "the."
5 "her" is possibly "his." But VB12r, ll. 9–10, suggests that "her" is more likely.
16 "bady" was probably intended as "baby."
a–c These lines are from the upper right margin and are revisions of ll. 1–5, VB11r, which they replace.

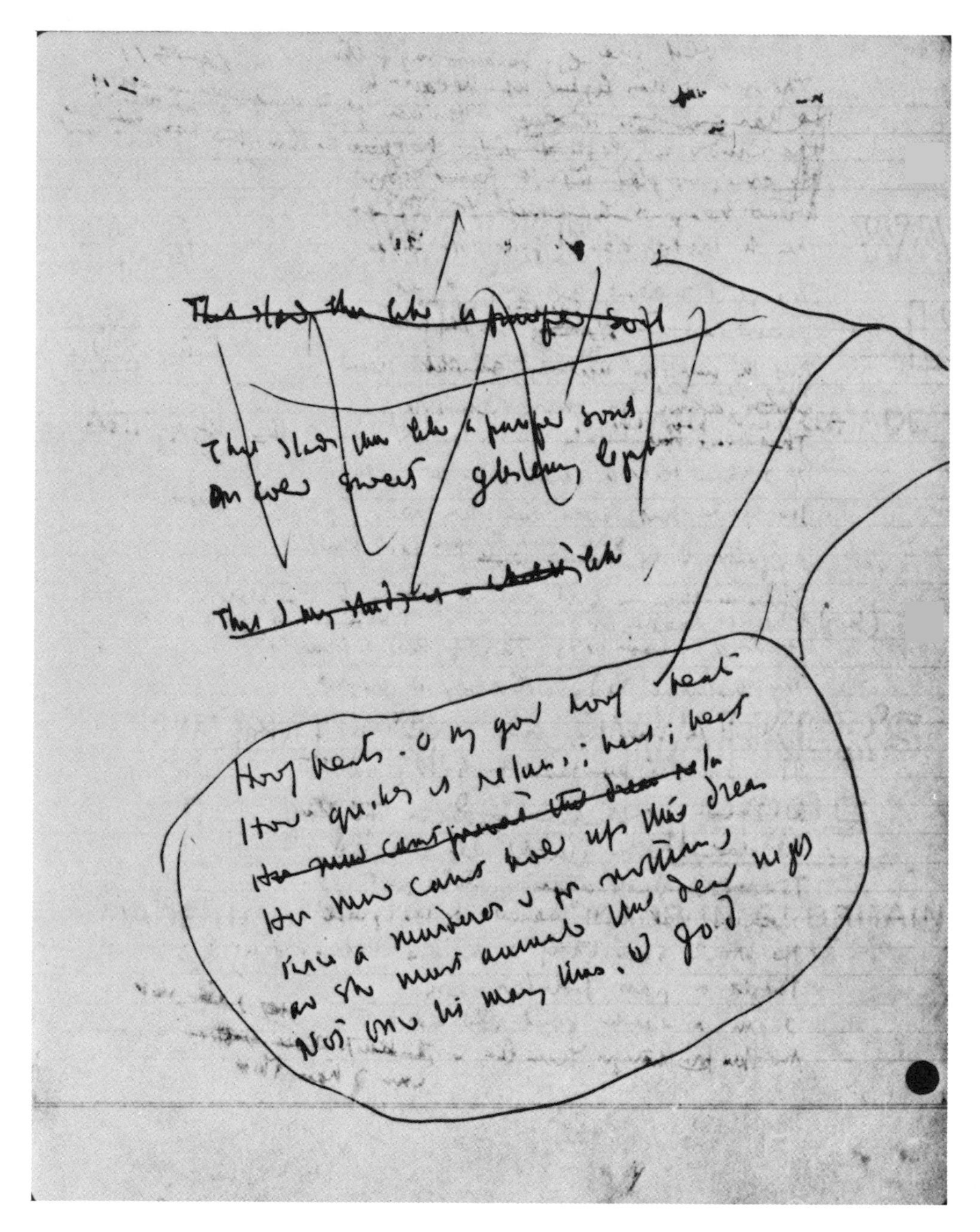

1 ~~That stands there like a purified soul~~

2 That stands there like a purified soul
3 All cold sweet glistening light

4 ~~That I might study it — what it~~ like

5 Hoof beats— O my God hoof beats
6 How quickly it returns; beat; beat
7 ~~Her mind cannot prevent that dream retu~~
8 Her mind cannot hold up that dream
9 Twice a murderer & for nothing
10 And she must animate that dead night
11 Not once but many times. O God

The directional lines connect with VB12r.
1–4 After adding ll. 9–11, these new lines were added to follow VB12r, l. 8.
5–11 These are revisions of ll. 10–14 on VB12r, which they replace.

1 ~~My jackknife~~
2 ~~My knife into~~ the
3 This old jackknife into a sod
~~Pull~~
4 And pulled it out all bright again
I ll all
5 And∧picked up ~~all~~ the money that he dropped
Hurry to
6 ~~I up~~∧to a distant place & there
~~Tell my~~
7 ~~I ll make old jokes among mew men~~

This leaf, which is unpaginated and is in black ink, was probably composed after Yeats reached l. 27, VB11^r, from which it continues, but before he made new revisions of the lines on VB12^r.

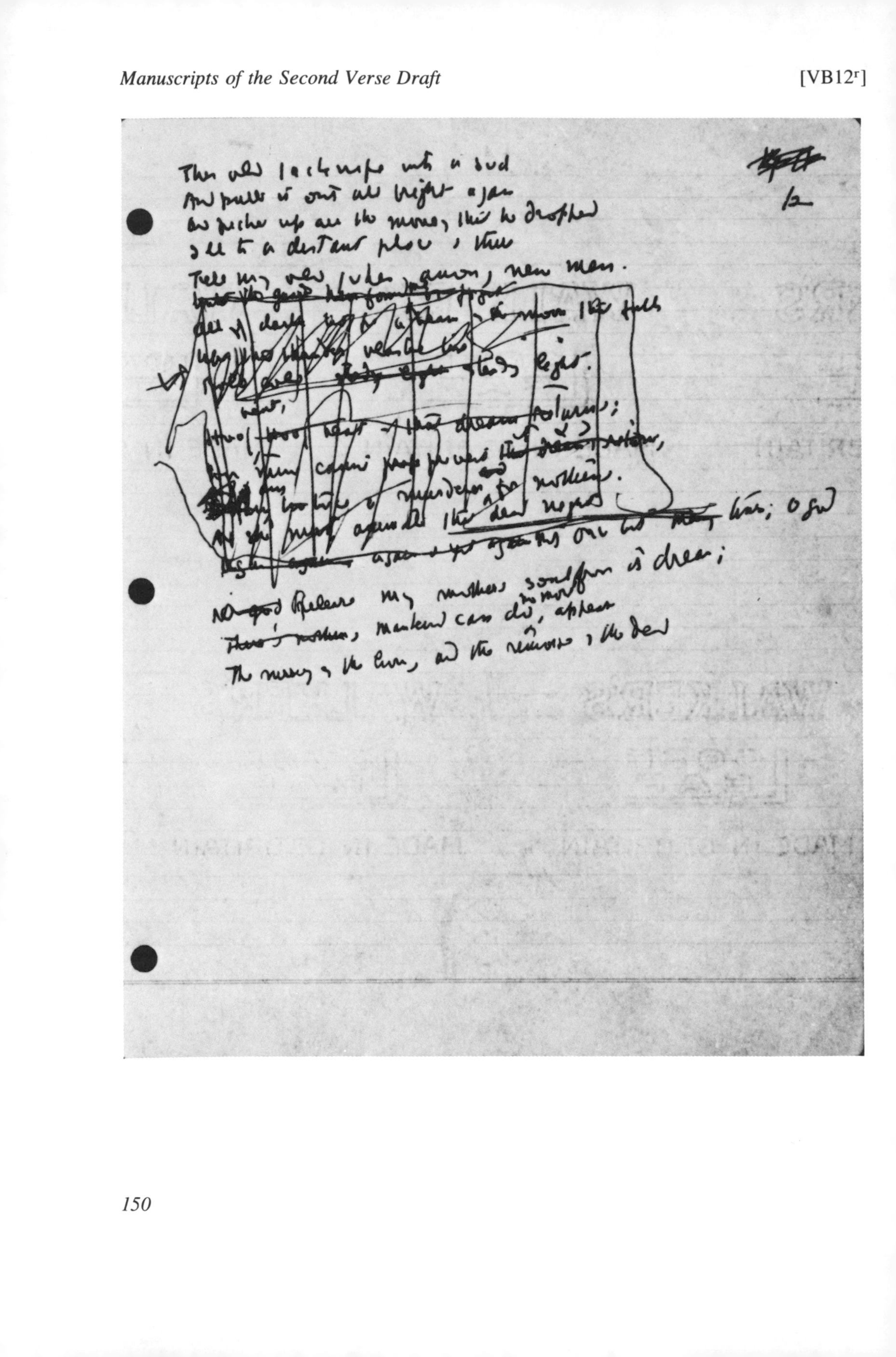

1 This old jacknife into a sod 14 11 12
2 And pulled it out all bright again
3 And picked up all the money that he dropped
4 I ll to a distant place & there
5 Tell my old jokes among new men.

me
6 Until the guards have found^or forget
7 All is dark but for a beam of the moon that falls
8 Upon that thunder blasted tree
9 Bold cold ~~steady light~~ steady light.

beats
10 Hoof^—Hoof beat— ~~that dream returns;~~

it & I
11 Her mind cannot ~~prefe~~ prevent ~~that dream returning~~

And I am ~~and~~
12 [? ? ?]^tw twice a murderer^for nothing.
13 And she must animate that dead night
14 ~~Again again~~ again & yet again Not once but many times; O God

R
15 ~~O God~~ release my mother s soul from its dream;

no more
16 ~~There's nothing~~ Mankind can do,^appease
17 The misery of the living and the remorse of the dead

6–9 These were to be replaced with ll. 10–14, which Yeats cancelled.
10–14 These were revised and replaced with VB11v, ll. 5–11.

Purgatory

TYPESCRIPTS

There are four typescript versions of *Purgatory* in folders in the National Library of Ireland MS 8771 #4, #5, #6, and #7. These numbers, however, represent neither the order in which the typescripts were prepared nor the order in which they were revised. TS6, which represents the earliest version, is on white wove paper measuring 25.3 × 20.3 cm and watermarked M/ABERMILL BOND/MADE IN GT BRITAIN. A black ribbon was used in typing this version, which is composed of a mixture of ribbon and carbon leaves; it has holograph revisions throughout in pencil and in blue-black ink in Yeats's hand. All versos are blank except 3^v, on which the carbon of 3^r is imprinted. Each page is marked "B" in pencil on the upper right margin; the letter "A" is similarly marked in pencil in the upper right margin of TS5, 1^r, and was probably inscribed there, as letters were inscribed on a few leaves of *The Death of Cuchulain* manuscript materials, by Curtis Bradford or by some other scholar. Yeats's corrections, revisions, and additions on TS6 were incorporated into a second typescript, National Library of Ireland MS 8771#4. All of the pages are black ribbon except page 2, which is carbon; all are on white wove paper measuring 25.4 cm × 20.4 cm and watermarked SWIFT BROOK/BOND. All versos are blank. There are holograph corrections in pencil in Yeats's hand. The entire typescript has been folded in half once horizontally and then folded once again. It also bears a crease mark from having been folded vertically in half. The typescripts in folders MSS 8771 #6 and #4 represent the earlier versions, corrections and revisions on which were incorporated into the two later typescripts contained in folders MSS 8771 #5 and #7.

Each of the unnumbered first page of TSS 5 and 7, and each of the numbered pages 2, 3, 4, and 5 are carbons made of the same ribbon copy. In the adjustment of the pagination to the longer typescript of *On the Boiler,* the numbers 52, 53, 54, 55, and 56 were inscribed in the upper right margin; the sixth, seventh, and eighth pages are carbons of a freshly prepared master and are paginated as 57, 58, and 59 in type rather than holograph. Both typescripts have corrections in Yeats's hand, although on TS7, which represents the later version, he introduced some new revisions. In addition, Mrs. Yeats transferred to TS7 the holograph revisions Yeats had made on pages 1, 2, and 3 of TS5. Both typescripts are on white wove paper measuring 24.4 cm × 20.4 cm and watermarked SWIFT BROOK/BOND. All versos on TS5 are blank except page 6^{v}, which contains a holograph insertion. In TS5 holograph revisions are in pencil and in blue-black ink in Yeats's hand. An "A" is written in pencil on the upper right margin of the first page of the typescript and is probably nonauthorial. There is, in addition, an odd holograph leaf belonging to *Purgatory* in a black ring binder marked "Book 74" on the inside front cover, in the possession of Senator Michael B. Yeats among the Cliff House papers in Dalkey. It is written on white wove looseleaf paper, punched with three holes and having a double red top margin rule. The paper measures 18.0 cm × 11.0 cm and is watermarked WALKERS/Loose Leaf/MADE IN GT BRITAIN. This leaf, which is written in blue ink, represents a later stage of revision intermediary between page 6^{r} and page 6^{v} of TS5. It is identified as TS5, $6i^{r}$. All versos of MS 8771#7 are blank. There are holograph revisions throughout in black ink and in pencil in Yeats's hand, and, on pages 52, 53, 55, and 56 there are seven lines that Mrs. Yeats transferred from Yeats's holograph revisions on TS5. In each of the seven lines (p. 52, l. 3, p. 53, l. 43, p. 55, ll. 92 and 93b, and p. 56, l. 137) there is a discrepancy in punctuation and, in one instance, a discrepancy between an upper and lower case letter. But in each of the lines Mrs. Yeats transferred with changes, excepting line 43, she corrected Yeats's obvious oversights. For example, in line 93b, Mrs. Yeats transcribed as an uppercase "E," which Yeats had neglected to change when he added the word "And" before "Everything" at the beginning of the sentence, to a lowercase "e"; and, in line 137, where Yeats neglected to cancel the repeated word "wall" and where the terminal punctuation is apparently absent in the line faintly inscribed in pencil, Mrs. Yeats dropped the unintended repetition and added a period at the end of the line. Each of these emendations is taken up in greater detail in *Notes on Textual Problems in TS7 and the Printed Versions*. Whether Mrs. Yeats introduced these changes with Yeats's knowledge or supervision is unclear. It should be pointed out, however, that when Yeats corrected page proofs he retained all of the changes Mrs. Yeats had introduced and which were printed as they appear in TS7. All, that is, except the uncertain terminal punctuation that Mrs. Yeats added. It is treated as a dash in the variants below, but on the page proofs it was printed as a period, which Yeats retained. There are no other holograph revisions on TS7 which were not also made on TS5. The typescript had been folded in half horizontally. In addition to the four typescripts contained in NLI MS8771, there is one page of typescript, also among the Cliff House papers, which is a carbon of page 7 of TS5 and has on it holograph insertions in the hands of Yeats and Mrs. Yeats. In the transcription that follows, it has been relocated in TS5 and identified as page $7s^{1}$. After Yeats revised page 7, which is itself a carbon, Mrs. Yeats copied the revisions he had made on a clean second carbon of page 7. But after seeing the clean copy, Yeats made further revisions on the second carbon. He then transferred those fresh revisions he wished to retain to the first carbon on which he then revised further. Some of those revisions on page $7s^{1}$ were imperfectly transferred to TS7.

Typescript leaves, and holograph leaves belonging with the typescript material, are identified by a page number. Leaves in the National Library of Ireland have been assigned a folder number: for example, TS5, 2^{r}, NLI MS 8771(5). Those in the collection of Senator Michael B. Yeats are followed by "MBY." A number, followed by a lowercase "i" indicates that the leaf is intermediary between two leaves of the typescript; a number followed by a lowercase "s" and the superscript "1" indicates that the leaf supercedes the carbon of that leaf. All leaves are identified as recto or verso pages. Identifications in the list that follows are provisional because of the difficulty of discerning whether a page is a ribbon copy or carbon.

TS4, 1^{r}	(ribbon)	NLI MS 8771(4)
TS4, 2^{r}	(ribbon)	NLI MS 8771(4)
TS4, 3^{r}	(carbon)	NLI MS 8771(4)
TS4, 4^{r}	(ribbon)	NLI MS 8771(4)
TS4, 5^{r}	(ribbon)	NLI MS 8771(4)
TS4, 6^{r}	(ribbon)	NLI MS 8771(4)
TS4, 7^{r}	(ribbon)	NLI MS 8771(4)
TS4, 8^{r}	(ribbon)	NLI MS 8771(4)
TS5, 1^{r}	(carbon)	NLI MS 8771(5)
TS5, 2^{r}	(carbon)	NLI MS 8771(5)
TS5, 3^{r}	(carbon)	NLI MS 8771(5)
TS5, 4^{r}	(carbon)	NLI MS 8771(5)
TS5, 5^{r}	(carbon)	NLI MS 8771(5)
TS5, 6^{r}	(carbon)	NLI MS 8771(5)
TS5, $6i^{r}$	(holograph)	MBY
TS5, 6^{v}	(holograph)	NLI MS 8771(5)
TS5, 7^{r}	(carbon)	NLI MS 8771(5)
TS5, $7s^{1r}$	(carbon)	MBY
TS5, 8^{r}	(carbon)	NLI MS 8771(5)
TS6, 1^{r}	(carbon)	NLI MS 8771(6)
TS6, 2^{r}	(ribbon)	NLI MS 8771(6)
TS6, 3^{r}	(ribbon)	NLI MS 8771(6)
TS6, 4^{r}	(ribbon)	NLI MS 8771(6)
TS6, 5^{r}	(carbon)	NLI MS 8771(6)
TS6, 6^{r}	(ribbon)	NLI MS 8771(6)
TS6, 7^{r}	(ribbon)	NLI MS 8771(6)
TS7, 1^{r}	(carbon)	NLI MS 8771(7)
TS7, 2^{r}	(carbon)	NLI MS 8771(7)
TS7, 3^{r}	(carbon)	NLI MS 8771(7)
TS7, 4^{r}	(carbon)	NLI MS 8771(7)
TS7, 5^{r}	(carbon)	NLI MS 8771(7)
TS7, 6^{r}	(carbon)	NLI MS 8771(7)
TS7, 7^{r}	(carbon)	NLI MS 8771(7)
TS7, 8^{r}	(carbon)	NLI MS 8771(7)

TS5: Transcriptions and Photographic Reproductions with Variants from TS6 and TS4

TS6 was prepared from the manuscript of MS 8771#3, probably by Mrs. Yeats under Yeats's supervision. At least one carbon was prepared, some pages of which were incorporated into TS4. Once TS6 had been prepared Yeats corrected it for typographical and other mechanical errors, cancelled some lines and added some new ones. TS4 incorporates the corrections and revisions Yeats made on TS6. He then turned to TS5, which contains some of the carbons of TS4 but also some freshly typed pages. All of the revisions that had been made on TS6 and TS4 were transferred to TS5, which Yeats then further revised. TS5 also contains new holograph additions that are more extensive than those on TS4 or TS6.

The cumulative effect of the revisions on TSS 6, 4, and 5 was to tighten the metric scheme and to perfect the four-beat line. One example occurs in line 2: ''Holding up this old pack'' was changed on TS4 to ''Hill or hollow, shouldering this pack.'' Another occurs in TS5, line 43: ''Sit down upon the stone, or I Will cut a stick out of that tree'' has been revised to: ''Stop; sit there upon that stone.'' Finally, also in TS5, line 124: ''There's nothing in the window, all there is black,'' has been revised to ''There's nothing but an empty gap in the wall.'' This last is not so much a matter of adjusting the metrical scheme, although it is that too, as an example of a revision in diction. The ''nothing''—that is, the ''empty gap''—is more richly suggestive than ''all is black.'' The phrase behaves rather like a picture puzzle that reveals a second shape if one squints hard enough: the meaning of that ''empty gap'' will soon be revealed. The revision of the Boy's lines here reflects more acutely than the unrevised line does that his denial is motivated by his fear that there *is* something horrible to be denied.

In the collations that follow, TS5, in its final form, is used as the basic text. Variant readings are from TSS 6 and 4. The abbreviations that follow are used in the variants:

TS6	TS6 where no revision has been made.
$TS6^1$	The unrevised reading of a variant in TS6 where revision has been made; where no further revision is indicated, the revised reading is identical to TS5.
$TS6^2$	TS6 where a variant is further revised.
$TS6^3$	TS6 where a third stage of revision has been made.
TS4	TS4 where no revision has been made.
$TS4^1$	The unrevised reading of a variant in TS4 where revision has been made; where no further revision is indicated, the revised reading is identical to TS5.
$TS4^2$	TS4 where a variant is further revised.

A

PURGATORY

(A ruined house and a bare tree in the background.)

BOY Half door, hall door
Hither and thither, day and night
~~Holding up this old pack~~ [Hill or hollow, shouldering this pack]
Hearing you talk.

OLD MAN Study that house.
I think about its jokes and stories;
I try to remember what the butler
Said to a drunken gamekeeper
In mid-October, but I cannot,
I cannot, and none living can.
Where are the jokes and stories of a house ,
Its threshold gone to patch a pig-stye?

BOY [So you have come this path before]
~~What do you know about this place~~?

OLD MAN The moonlight falls upon the path,
The shadow of a cloud upon the house
And that symbolical; study that tree,
What is it like?

BOY A silly old man.

OLD MAN It's like - no matter what it's like.
I saw it a year ago stripped bare as now,
I saw it fifty years ago
Before the thunder-belt had riven it,
Green leaves, ripe leaves, leaves thick as butter,
Fat, greasy life. Stand there and look,
Because there is somebody in that house.

(The BOY puts down pack and stands in the doorway)

BOY There's nobody here.

OLD MAN There's somebody there.

A

PURGATORY

(A ruined house and a bare tree~~e~~ in the background.)

1 BOY Half door, hall door
2 Hither and thither, day and night,
3 ~~Holding up this old pack~~ Hill or hollow, shouldering this pack
4a Hearing you talk.
4b OLD MAN ~~Study that house.~~ Study that house.
5 I think about its jokes and stories;
6 I try to remember what the butler
7 Said to a drunken gamekeeper
8 In mid-October, but I cannot,
9 I cannot, and none living can.
10 Where are the jokes and stories of a house ,
11 Its threshold gone to patch a pig-stye?
So you have come this path before
12 BOY ~~What do you know about this place~~?
13 OLD MAN The moonlight falls upon the path,
14 The shadow of a cloud upon the house
15 And that symbolical; study that tree,
16a What is it like?
16b BOY ~~A silly old man.~~ A silly old man.
17 OLD MAN It's like—no matter what it's like.
18 I saw it a year ago stripped bare as now,
19 I saw it fifty years ago
20 Before the thunder-bolt had riven it,
21 Green leaves, ripe leaves, leaves thick as butter,
22 Fat, greasy life. Stand there and look,
23 Because there is somebody in that house.
(The BOY puts down pack and stands in the doorway)
24 BOY There's nobody here.
OLD MAN There's somebody there.

2

BOY The floor is gone, the windows gone,
And where there should be roof there's sky,
And here's a bit of an egg-shell thrown
Out of a jackdaw's nest.

OLD MAN But there are some
That do not care what's gone, what's left,
The souls in Purgatory that come back
To habitations and familiar spots.

BOY Your wits are out again.

OLD MAN Re-live
Their transgressions, and that not once
But many times, they know at last
The consequence of those transgressions
Whether upon others or upon themselves;
If upon others, others may bring help
For when the consequence is at an end
The dream must end; if upon themselves
There is no help but in themselves
And in the mercy of God.

BOY I have had enough!
Talk to the jackdaws, if talk you must.

(in gown)

OLD MAN ~~Sit down upon this stone, or I~~
~~will cut a stick out of [illegible]~~ Stop; but [illegible] upon that stone

That is the house where I was born.

BOY The big old house that was burnt down?

OLD MAN My mother that was your grand-dam owned it,
This scenery and this countryside,
Kennel and stable, horse and hound -

She had a horse at the Curragh, and there met
My father, a groom in a training stable;
Looked at him and married him.
Her mother never spoke to ~~him~~ her again,
And she did right.

2

25 BOY The floor is gone, the windows gone,
26 And where there should be roof there's sky,
27 And here's a bit of an egg-shell thrown
28 Out of a jackdaw's nest.
OLD MAN But there are some
29 That do not care what's gone, what's left,
30 The souls in Purgatory that come back
31 To habitations and familiar spots.
32 BOY Your wits are out again.
OLD MAN Re-live
33 Their transgressions, and that not once
34 But many times, they know at last
35 The consequence of those transgressions
36 Whether upon others or upon themselves;
37 If upon others, others may bring help
38 For when the consequence is at an end
39 The dream must end; if upon themselves
40 There is no help but in themselves
41 And in the mercy of God.
BOY I have had enough!
42 Talk to the jackdaws, if talk you must.
(is going)
43 OLD MAN [~~Sit down upon this stone, or I~~ Stop; sit there upon that stone
44 ~~Will cut a stick out of that tree~~.
45 That is the house where I was born.
46 BOY The big old house that was burnt down?
47 OLD MAN My mother that was your grand-dam owned it,
48 This scenery and this countryside,
49 Kennel and stable, horse and hound—
50 She had a horse at the Curragh, and there met
51 My father, a groom in a training stable;
52 Looked~~a~~ at him and married him.
53 Her mother never spoke to ~~him~~ again, *her/*
54 And she did right

3

BOY What's right and wrong?
My grand-dad got the girl and the money.

OLD MAN Looked at him and married him,
And he squandered everything she had.

She never knew the worst, because
She died in giving birth to me,
But now she knows it all, being dead.

Great people lived and died in this house;
Magistrates, colonels, members of Parliament,
Captains and governors, and long ago
Men that had fought at Aughrim and the Boyne.
Some that had gone on government work
To London or to India came home to die,
Or came from London every spring
To look at the May-blossom in the park.
They had loved the trees that he cut down
To pay what he had lost at cards
Or spent on horses, drink and women;
Had loved the house, had loved all
The intricate passages of the house,
But he killed the house; to kill a house
Where great men grew up, married, died,
I here declare a capital offence.

BOY My God, but you had luck. Grand clothes,
And maybe a grand horse to ride.

OLD MAN That he might keep me upon his level
He never sent me to school, but some
Half-loved me for my half of her,
A gamekeeper's wife taught me to read,
A Catholic curate taught me Latin.
There were old books and books made fine
By eighteenth century French binding, books
Modern and ancient, books by the ton.

BOY What education have you given me?

3

BOY What's right and wrong?
55 My grand-dad got the girl and the money.
56 OLD MAN. Looked at him and married him,
57 And he squandered everything she had.
58 She never knew the worst, because
59 She died in giving birth to me,
60 But now she knows it all, being dead.
61 Great people lived and died in this house;
62 Magistrates, colonels, members of Parliament,
63 Captains and governors, and long ago
64 Men that had fought at Aughrim and the Boyne.
65 Some that had gone on government work
66 To London or to India came home to die,
67 Or came from London every spring
68 To look at the May-blossom in the park.
69 They had loved the trees that he cut down
70 To pay what he had lost at cards
71 Or spent on horses, drink and women;
72 Had loved the house, had loved all
73 The intricate passages of the house,
74 But he killed the house; to kill a house
75 Where great men grew up, married, died,
76 I here declare a capital offence.
77 BOY My God, but you had luck. Grand clothes,
78 And maybe a grand horse to ride.
79 OLD MAN That he might keep me upon his level
80 He never sent me to school, but some
81 Half-loved me for my half of her,
82 A gamekeeper's wife taught me to read,
83 A Catholic curate taught me Latin.
84 There were old books and books made fine
85 By eighteenth century French bindings, books
86 Modern and ancient, books by the ton.
87 BOY What education have you given me?

4

OLD MAN I gave the education that befits
A bastard that a peddlar got
Upon a tinker's daughter in a ditch.

When I had ~~reached my fifteenth~~ come into my sixteenth year
My father burned down the house when drunk.

BOY ~~Then on my birthday~~ But that is my age, sixteen years old
~~And that's my age?~~ At the Puck Fair,

OLD MAN And everything was burnt;
Books, library, all were burnt.

BOY Is what I have heard upon the road the truth,
That you killed him in the burning house?

OLD MAN There's nobody here but our two selves?

BOY Nobody, Father.

OLD MAN I stuck him with a knife,
That knife that cuts my dinner now,
And after that I left him in the fire;
They dragged him out, somebody saw
The knife-wound but could not be certain
Because the body was all black and charred.
Then some that were his drunken friends
Swore they would put me upon trial,
Spoke of quarrels, a threat I had made.
The gamekeeper gave me some old clothes,
I ran away, worked here and there
Till I became a pedlar on the roads,
No good trade, but good enough
Because I am my father's son,
Because of what I did or may do.

Listen to the hoof beats! Listen, listen!

BOY I cannot hear a sound.

4

88 OLD MAN **I gave the education that befits**
89 **A bastard that a peddlar got**
90 **Upon a tinker's daughter in a ditch.**
come into my sixteenth
91 **When I had ~~reached my fifteenth~~ year**
92 **My father burned down the house when drunk.**
But that is my age, sixteen years old /
~~This is my birthday, that's my age~~
93a BOY **~~And that's my age.~~**
~~Sixteen to day~~ ~~on Gort Fair Day~~. At the Puck Fair^
93b OLD MAN ^**Everything was burnt;** And^
94 **Books, library, all were burnt.**
95 BOY **Is what I have heard upon the road the truth,**
96 **That you killed him in the burning house?**
97 OLD MAN **There's nobody here but our two selves?**
98 BOY **Nobody, Father.**
OLD MAN **I stuck him with a knife,**
99 **That knife that cuts my dinner now,**
100 **And after that I left him in the fire;**
101 **They dragged him out, somebody saw**
102 **The knife-wound but could not be certain**
103 **Because the body was all black and charred.**
104 **Then some that were his drunken friends**
105 **Swore they would put me upon trial,**
106 **Spoke of quarrels, a threat I had made.**
107 **The gamekeeper gave me some old clothes,**
108 **I ran away, worked here and there**
109 **Till I became a pedlar on the roads,**
110 **No good trade, but good enough**
111 **Because I am my father's son,**
112 **Because of what I did or may do.**
113 **Listen to the hoof beats! Listen, listen!**
114 BOY **I cannot hear a sound.**

5

OLD MAN Beat! Beat!
This night is the anniversary
Of my mother's wedding night,
Or of the night wherein I was begotten.
My father is riding from the public house
A whiskey bottle under his arm.

(a window is lit, showing a young girl)

Look at the window; she stands there
Listening, the servants are all in bed,
She is alone, he has stayed late
Bragging and drinking in the public house.

There's nothing but an empty gap in the wall

BOY ~~There's nothing in the window, all there is black,~~
You have made it up. No, you are mad!
You are getting madder every day.

OLD MAN It's louder now because he rides
Upon a gravelled avenue
All grass today. The hoof beat stops,
He has gone to the other side of the house
To put the horse up. All that is hidden
But I can see it all in the mind.
She has gone down to open the door.
This night she is no better than her man
And does not mind that he is half drunk,
She is mad about him. They mount the stairs
She brings him into her own chamber. ~~Now~~
Range The window is dimly lit again.
~~Because she has put the candle upon the table~~
~~And the passage door is open; now~~
~~That door is shut and the window dark.~~

O do not let him touch you! It is not true
That drunken men cannot beget
And if he touch he must beget
And you must bear his murderer.

Deaf! Both deaf! If I shoud throw
A stick or a stone they would not hear;
And that's a proof my wits are out.
But here's a problem: she must live

~~That is now~~ And there is the marriage chamber. Now

OLD MAN Beat! Beat!
115 This night is the anniversary
116 Of my mother's wedding night,
117 Or of the night wherein I was begotten.
118 My father is riding from the public house
119 A whiskey bottle under his arm.
(a window is lit, showing a young girl)
120 Look at the window; she stands there
121 Listening, the servants are all in bed,
122 She is alone, he has stayed late
123 Bragging and drinking in the public house.
There is nothing but an empty gap in the wall wall
124 BOY ~~There's nothing in the window, all there is black~~,
125 You have made it up. No, you are mad!
126 You are getting madder every day.
127 OLD MAN It's louder now because he rides
128 Upon a gravelled avenue
129 All grass today. The hoof beats stops,
130 He has gone to the other side of the house
131 To put the horse up. All that is hidden
132 But I can see it all in the mind.
133 She has gone down to open the door.
134 This night she is no better than her man
135 And does not mind that he is half drunk,
136 She is mad about him. They mount the stairs
137 She brings him into her own chamber. ~~Now~~
138 *Range* The window is dimly lit again
139 ~~Because she has put the candle upon the table~~
140 And the passage door is open; now
141 That door is shut and the window dark.
142 O do not let him touch you! It is not true
143 That drunken men cannot beget
144 And if he touch he must beget
145 And you must bear his murderer.
146 Deaf! Both deaf! If I shoud throw
147 A stick or a stone they would not hear;
148 And that's a proof my wits are out.
149 But here's a problem: she must live

is
137a ~~That is now~~ And that ^ the marriage chamber. now

6

OLD MAN Through everything in exact detail,
Driven to it by remorse, and yet
Can she renew the sexual act
And find no pleasure in it, and if not
If pleasure and remorse must both be there
Which is the greater?
I lack schooling.
Go fetch Tertullian; he and I
Will ravel all that problem out
Whilst those two lie upon the mattress
Begetting me.
Come back! Come back!
And so you thought to slip away,
My bag of money in your fingers, between
And that I could not talk and see!

You have been rummaging in the pack.

(the light in the window has faded out)

BOY You kept it all and never gave me a share.

OLD MAN And had I given it, young as you are
You would have spent it upon drink.

BOY What if I did? I had a right
To get my share and spend it as I chose.

OLD MAN Give me that bag and no more words.

BOY What if I kill you? You killed my grand-dad
Because you were young and he was old,
And now I am young and you are old.

(The OLD MAN knocks the boy down, the purse falls and the money rolls out.)

OLD MAN Pick up that money and stand up.

BOY (picking up money) and half rises,
Knocked about, Ordered about!

(window lit up. A man is seen pouring whiskey into a glass

150	OLD MAN	Through everything in exact detail,	6
151		Driven to it by remorse, and yet	
152		Can she renew the sexual act	
153		And find no pleasure in it, and if not	
154		If pleasure and remorse must both be there	
155		Which is the greater?	
		I lack schooling.	
156		Go fetch Tertullian; he and I	
157		Will ravel all that problem out	
158		Whilst those two lie upon the mattress	
159		Begetting me.	
		Come back! Came back!	
160		And so you thought to slip away,	
161		My bag of money ~~in~~ *between* / your fingers,	
162		And that I could not talk and see!	
163		You have been rummaging in the pack.	
		(the light in the window has faded out)	
164	BOY	You kept it all and never gave me a share.	
165	OLD MAN	And had I given it, young as you are	
166		You would have spent it upon drink.	
			see back
167	BOY	What if I did? I had a right	
168		To get my share and spend it as I chose.	
169	OLD MAN	Give me that bag and no more words.	
170	BOY	What if I kill you? You killed my grand-dad	
171		Because you were young and he was old,	
172		And now I am young and you are old.	
		(The OLD MAN knocks the boy down, the purse falls and the money rolls out.)	
173	OLD MAN	Pick up that money and stand up.	
	BOY	(picking up money) *and half rising*	
174		Knocked about, ordered about!	
		(window~~s~~ lit up. A man is seen pouring whiskey into a glass)	

Window is lit up man is seen pouring
whiskey into a glass

Old Man

sixteen

174a younger better looking [?for] ~~fifteen~~ years

Boy

174b What are you muttering

Old Ma

174c She might have known

174d ~~Th~~[?] she might have known the [?difference]

Boy

174e What are you saying—out with it
(Old Man points to window)

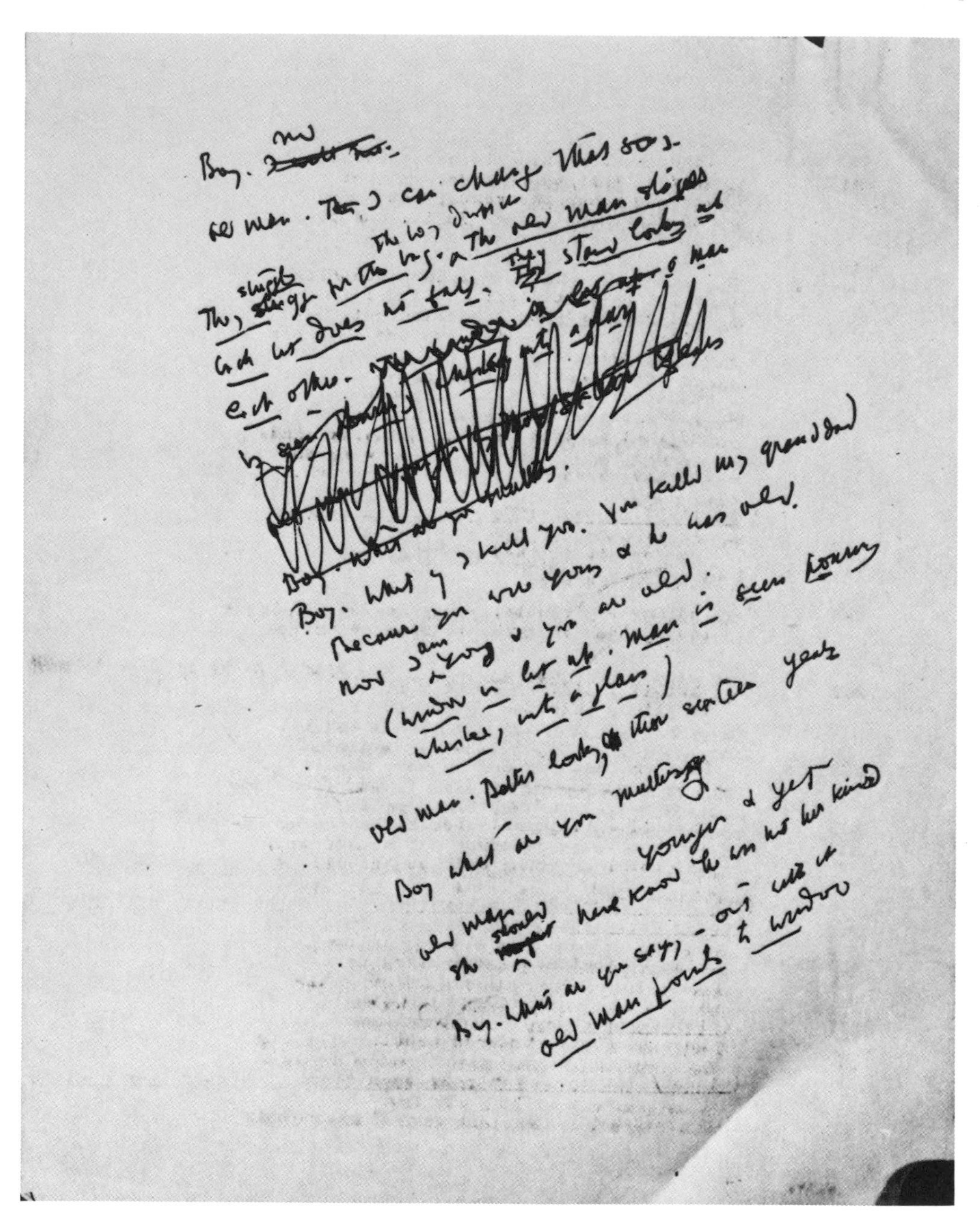

169a No
Boy. ~~I will no~~t.
169b Old man. ~~Then~~ I can change that song.
struggle The boy drops it
They ~~strugg~~ for the bag.^The Old Man staggers
They
back but does not fall. ~~Th~~ stand looking at
each other. ~~The window is lit up.~~ A man
~~is seen pouring whiskey into a glass~~
169c ~~Old Man. Young [?] those sixteen years~~
169d ~~Boy. What are you muttering~~.
169e Boy. What if I kill you. You killed my granddad
169f Because you were young & he was old.
am
169g Now I^young & you are old.
(window is lit up. Man is seen pouring
whiskey into a glass)
169h Old Man. Better looking ~~all~~ those sixteen years
169i Boy What are you muttering
169j Old Man Younger & yet
should
She ~~might~~^have known he was not her kind
169k Boy. What are you saying out with it
Old Man points to window

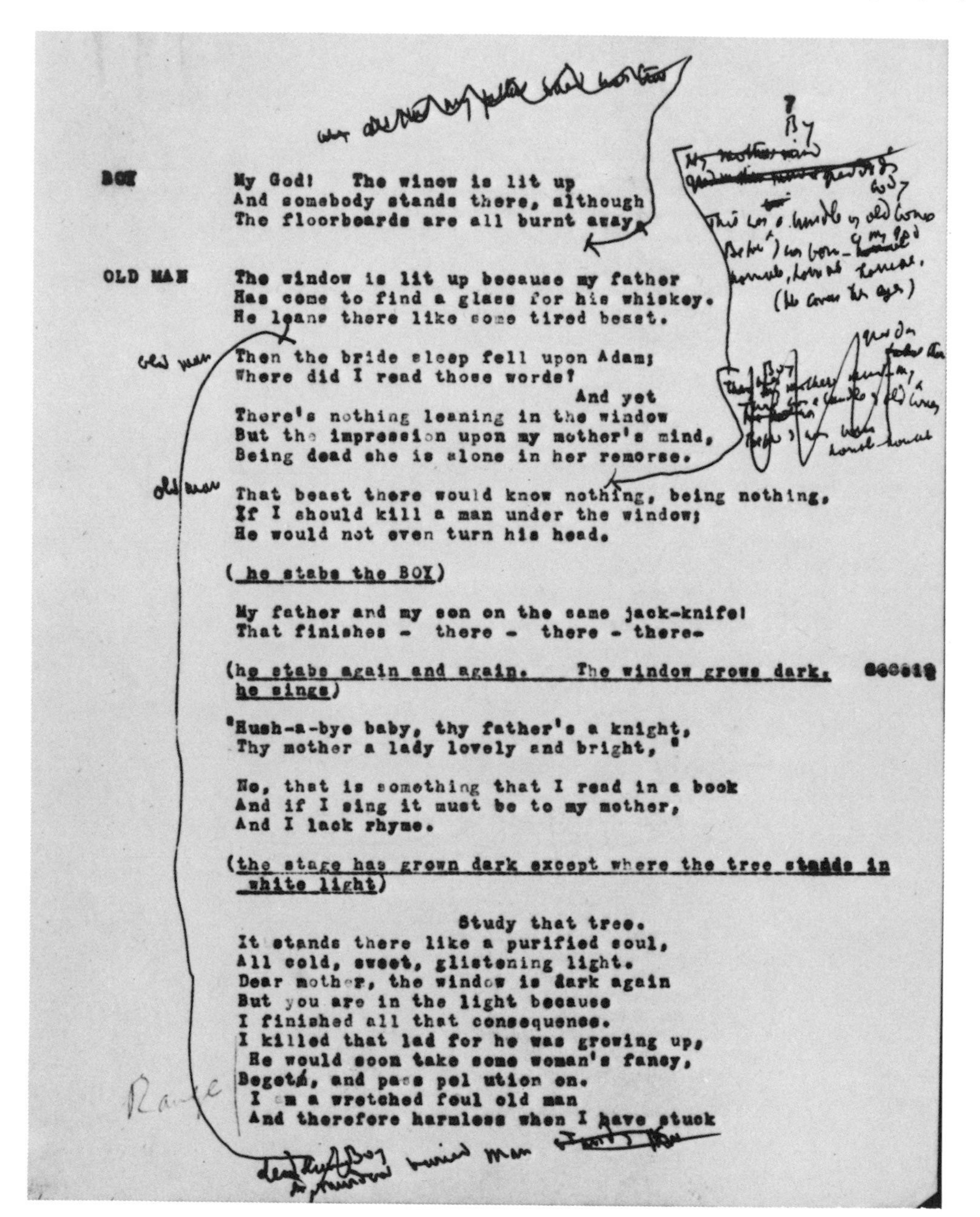

BOY My God! The winow is lit up
And somebody stands there, although
The floorboards are all burnt away.

OLD MAN The window is lit up because my father
Has come to find a glass for his whiskey.
He leans there like some tired beast.

Then the bride sleep fell upon Adam;
Where did I read those words?
And yet
There's nothing leaning in the window
But the impression upon my mother's mind,
Being dead she is alone in her remorse.

That beast there would know nothing, being nothing,
If I should kill a man under the window;
He would not even turn his head.

(he stabs the BOY)

My father and my son on the same jack-knife!
That finishes - there - there - there-

(he stabs again and again. The window grows dark. he sings)

"Hush-a-bye baby, thy father's a knight,
Thy mother a lady lovely and bright,"

No, that is something that I read in a book
And if I sing it must be to my mother,
And I lack rhyme.

(the stage has grown dark except where the tree stands in white light)

Study that tree.
It stands there like a purified soul,
All cold, sweet, glistening light.
Dear mother, the window is dark again
But you are in the light because
I finished all that consequence.
I killed that lad for he was growing up,
He would soon take some woman's fancy,
Beget, and pass pollution on.
I am a wretched foul old man
And therefore harmless when I have stuck

7

177a ~~All All that my father said was true~~
175 BOY My God! The winow is lit up
176 And somebody stands there, although
177 The floorboards are all burnt away.
178 OLD MAN The window is lit up because my father
179 Has come to find a glass for his whiskey.
180 He leans there like some tired beast.
181 Old Man Then the bride sleep fell upon Adam;
182 Where did I read those words?
And yet
183 There's nothing leaning in the window
184 But the impression upon my mother's mind,
185 Being dead she is alone in her remorse.
186 Old Man That beast there would know nothing, being nothing,
187 If I should kill a man under the window;
188 He would not even turn his head.
(he stabs the BOY)
189 My father and my son on the same jack-knife!
190 That finishes—there—there—there—
(he stabs again and again. The window grows dark. @@@@@@
he sings)
191 "Hush-a-bye baby, thy father's a knight,
192 Thy mother a lady lovely and bright,"
193 No, that is something that I read in a book
194 And if I sing it must be to my mother,
195a And I lack rhyme.
(the stage has grown dark except where the tree stands in
white light)
195b Study that tree.
196 It stands there like a purified soul,
197 All cold, sweet, glistening light.
198 Dear mother, the window is dark again
199 But you are in the light because
200 I finished all that consequence.
201 I killed that lad for he was growing up,
202 He would soon take some woman's fancy,
203 Begetm, and pass pol ution on.
204 *Range* I am a wretched foul old man
205 And therefore harmless when I have stuck
Boy
180a dead living
A murdered buried man ~~stands there~~

Boy
185a ~~My mother s mind~~
185b ~~Grandmothers mind & granddad's~~
body
~~but~~
185c That was∧a bundle of old bones
O my god
185d Before I was born— ~~horrible~~

185e Horrible, horrible horrible.
(He covers his eyes)

Boy grandam
~~They~~ Her
~~father~~ that
185f ~~my~~ mothers mind—my^
185g That was a bundle of old bones
~~He that was~~
185h Before I was born
185i horrible—horrible

7 *58*

175	BOY	**My God! The winow is lit up**
176		**And somebody stands there, although**
177		**The floorboards are all burnt away.**
178	OLD MAN	**The window is lit up because my father**
179		**Has come to find a glass for his whiskey.**
180		**He leans there like some tired beast.**
181	Old Man	**Then the bride sleep fell upon Adam;**
182		**Where did I read those words?**
		And yet
183		**There's nothing leaning in the window**
184		**But the impression upon my mother's mind,**
185		**Being dead she is alone in her^remorse.**
186	Old Man	**That beast there would know nothing, being nothing,**
187		**If I should kill a man under the window;**
188		**He would not even turn his head.**
		(he stabs the BOY)
189		**My father and my son on the same jack-knife!**
190		**That finishes—there—there—there—**
		(he stabs again and again. The window grows dark. @@@@@@ **he sings)**
191		**"Hush-a-bye baby, thy father's a knight,**
192		**Thy mother a lady lovely and bright,"**
193		**No, that is something that I read in a book**
194		**And if I sing it must be to my mother,**
195a		**And I lack rhyme.**
		(the stage has grown dark except where the tree stands in white light)
195b		**Study that tree.**
196		**It stands there like a purified soul,**
197		**All cold, sweet, glistening light.**
198		**Dear mother, the window is dark again**
199		**But you are in the light because**
200		**I finished all that consequence.**
201		**I killed that lad for he was growing up,**
202		**He would soon take some woman's fancy,**
203		**Begetm, and pass pol ution on.**
204	*Range*	**I am a wretched foul old man**
205		**And therefore harmless when I have stuck**

185a[1] *Boy. A body that was a bundle of old bones*
Horrible Horrible.
185b[1] *Before I was born.* ~~*O my God*~~
185c[1] ~~*Horrible, horrible, horrible.*~~
(He covers his eyes)
Boy
185d[1] Grandmother's mind and
185e[1] granddads body
185f[1] That was but a bundle of old bones
185g[1] Before I was born—O my God!
185h[1] Horrible, horrible horrible!
(He covers his eyes.)
180a[1] youn dead, living
Boy: A^murdered^~~buried~~ man stands there.

8

OLD MAN

This old jack-knife into a sod
And pulled it out all bright again,
And picked up all th money that he dropped
I'll to a distant place, and there
Tell my old jokes among new men.

(He cleans the knife and begins to pick up money)

Hoof beats! Dear God
How quickly it returns- beat - beat-

Her mind cannot hold up that dream.

Twice a murderer and all for nothing,
And she must animate that dead night
Not once but many times!
O God!
Release my mother's soul from its dream!
Mankind can do no more. Appease
The misery of the living and the remorse of the dead.

Range

8

206 OLD MAN This old jack-knife into a sod
207 And pulled it out all bright again,
208 And picked up all th money that he dropped
209 I'll to a distant place, and there
210 Tell my old jokes among new men.
(He cleans the knife and begins to pick up money)
211 Hoof beats! Dear God
212 How quickly it returns—beat—beat—
213 Her mind cannot hold up that dream.
214 Twice a murderer and all for nothing,
215 And she must animate that dead night
216 Not once but many times!
O God!
217 *Range* Release my mother's soul from its dream!
218 Mankind can do no more. Appease
219 The misery of the living and the remorse of
the dead.

Variants

Directions before 1 background, the house in shadow, the foreground and tree lit by the moon. *TS6* back-ground, *TS6*^{1}

1 door] door, *TS4*

2 thither,] thither *TS6* thirther *TS4*^{1} thither *TS4*^{2} night,] night *TS6, TS4*

3 Holding up this old pack *TS6, TS4*

4 talk.] talk *TS6*

5 stories;] stories *TS6*^{1}

6 butler] bulter *TS6*

8 cannot,] cannot *TS6*^{1}

10 house,] house *TS6*^{1}

12 What do you know about this place? *TS6, TS4*^{1} So you have come this path before. *TS4*^{2}

13 path,] path *TS6*^{1}

17 It's] Its *TS4*^{1} it's] its *TS6, TS4*^{1} like.] like *TS6*^{1} like, *TS4*

18 now,] now *TS6*

20 thunder-bolt] thunder *TS6*^{1} thunder bolt *TS6*^{2} it,] it *TS6*^{1}

21 butter,] butter *TS6*

22 Fat,] Fat *TS6, TS4* look,] look *TS6, TS4*

23 house.] house *TS6*

Directions after 23 doorway.) *TS4*

24 there.] in that house. *TS6*^{1}

25 windows gone,] windows gone *TS6*

29 left,] left *TS6*^{1}

32 out] gone *TS4*

39 If *TS6*^{1}

41a *lacking in TS6*^{1} and in the mercy of God— *TS6*^{2} God.] God— *TS4*

41b enough!] enough *TS6* enough. *TS4*

42 jackdaws,] jackdaws *TS4*

Directions after 42 (is going)] *lacking in TS6, TS4*

43 Sit down upon this stone or I *TS6, TS4*

44 Will cut a stick out of that tree. *TS4, also TS6 but* tree~~s~~.

45 born.] born *TS6*^{1}

46 *lacking in TS6*^{1} The old House that was all burnt down? *TS6*^{2} The big old House that was burnt down? *TS6*^{3} burnt] burned *TS4*

48 countryside,] countryside *TS6*^{1}

49 Kennerl *TS6*^{1} hound—] hound *TS6*^{1} hound. *TS4*

50 Curragh,] Curragh *TS6, TS4*

51 stable;] stable *TS6*^{1}

52 at him, *TS4*

53 again,] again *TS6, TS4*

55 got girl and money. *TS6*^{1}

56 married him,] married him *TS6*

57 had.] had *TS6*^{1}

61 house;] house *TS6*^{1} house, *TS6*^{2}*, TS4*

62 Colonels, *TS4*^{1} Parliament,] Parliament *TS6, TS4*

66 India, *TS4* die,] die *TS6*

68 park.] Park *TS6*^{1} Park. *TS6*^{2}*, TS4*

70 cards, *TS4*

71 women, *TS6*

73 house,] house *TS6*

74 house;] house, *TS6*
76 offence.] offence *TS6*
77 luck! *TS4* clothes,] clothes *TS6*
78 ride.] ride *TS6*
81 her,] her *TS6*^{1}
82 game-keeper's *TS6, TS4*
83 Latin.] Latin *TS6*^{1}
84 old books, *TS4*
89 pedlar *TS6, TS4*
90 ditch.] ditch *TS6*^{1}
91 When I had reached my fifteenth year *TS6, TS4*
92 burned down the house] set it upon fire *TS6*^{1} burned the house *TS6*^{2} burned down the house *TS6*^{3} drunk.] drunk *TS6*
93a And that's my age. *TS6, TS4*
93b The house was burnt *TS6*^{1} Everything was burnt; *TS6*^{2} Everything was burnt; *TS4*
94 burnt.] burnt *TS6*^{1}
95 And is it true what people say *TS6*^{1} And is it true what I have heard upon the road. *TS6*^{2} roads. *TS6*^{3}*, TS4, but TS6*^{3} *further revised to correspond to TS5*
97 selves?] selves *TS6*
98 knife,] knife *TS6*^{1}
99 now,] now *TS6*^{1}
100 left] dropped *TS6*^{1} fire;] fire *TS6*^{1} fire. *TS6*^{2}*, TS4*
105 trial,] trial *TS6*^{1}
106 made, *TS6*^{1}
107 The] But the *TS6*^{1} game-keeper *TS6, TS4* clothes,] clothes *TS6*
109 becamse *TS6* roads,] roads *TS6*^{1} roads; *TS4*
110 trade,] trade *TS6*
111 son,] son *TS6*
112 or] and *TS6*^{1}
113 beats, listen, listen! *TS6* beats! Listen, Listen! *TS4*
114 Beat, beat! *TS6, TS4*
116 night,] night *TS6*^{1}
117 Or of] Of *TS4* begotten.] begotten *TS6*^{1} begotten; *TS4*
118 the] a *TS6*^{1}
119 arm.] arm *TS6*
Directions after 119 (A window *TS6, TS4* lit,] lit *TS6, TS4* girl who stands listening) *TS6*^{1} girl.) *TS6*^{2}
120 window, *TS6*
121 bed,] bed *TS6*^{1}
123 house.] house *TS6*^{1}
124 There's nothing in the window, all there is black *TS6*^{1}*, also TS6*^{2}*, TS4 except* black,
125 No,] Np, *TS4*
126 day.] day *TS6*
127 That sound is louder, for it bea s *TS6*^{1} Its louder now, for the hoof-beat's *TS6*^{2} Its louder now, because he rides *TS6*^{3}
129 stops,] stops *TS6*^{1}
130 house] ouse *TS6*^{1}
132 mind.] mind *TS6*^{1}
133 door.] door *TS6*^{1} door, *TS4*
135 drunk,] drunk *TS6*
136 Because she is mad about him, They mount *TS6*^{1} She is mad about him, They mount the stairs; *TS6*^{2} mad] made *TS4*^{1} stairs; *TS4*
137 chamber.] chamber *TS6, TS4* Now *TS6, TS4*
137a And] For *TS6, TS4*
139 Because she has put the candle upon the table *TS6, TS4*
140 And the passage door is open; now *TS6, TS4*^{1}
141 That door is shut and the window dark. *TS6, TS4*^{1}
143 beget, *TS4*
146 Deaf, both deaf; if *TS6* shoud] should *TS6, TS4*
147 hear;] hear *TS6*^{1}

148 out.] out *TS6*
150 detail,] detail *TS6[1]*
155 Whiach *TS4* schooling.] schooling *TS6* schooling; *TS4*
156 Tertullian: *TS4*
159 Come back! Came back!] Come back! Come back! *TS6, TS4*
160 away,] away *TS6, TS4*
161 money in your *TS6, TS4* fingers,] fingers *TS6, TS4*
162 see. *TS6, TS4*
163 pack.] pack *TS6[1]*
Directions after 163 The *TS6, TS4* out. *TS6*
166 drink.] drink *TS6[1]*
169a–k and directions after 169k *lacking in TS6, TS4*
170 Grandad. *TS6[1]* grandad, *TS6[2]* grand-dad, *TS4*
171 old,] old *TS6*
172 old.] old *TS6[1]*
Directions after 172 BOY *TS6, TS4* down; *TS4* out.] out *TS6, TS4*
Directions in 174 and half rising *lacking in TS6, TS4*
174 ordered about. *TS6*
174a–e and direction after 174e *lacking in TS6, TS4*
Directions after 174 Windows *TS6, TS4*
175 window *TS6, TS4*
177a *lacking in TS6, TS4*
179 whiskey.] whiskey *TS6*
180 He leans there like some tired beast.] He, leaning there, looks like some tired beast *TS6[1] revised to TS5 but* beast *TS6[2]*
180a *lacking in TS6, TS4*
180a[1] *lacking in TS6, TS4*
181 Adam: *TS6[1], TS4*
184 mind,] mind *TS6[1]*
185 remorse.] remorse *TS6[1]*
185a–i *lacking in TS6, TS4*
185a[1]–h[1] *lacking in TS6, TS4*
187 window;] window *TS6[1]* window: *TS4* Directions after 188 (he stabs the BOY)] (He stabs BOY. The window goes dark) *TS6[1]* (He stabs BOY.) *TS6[2]* (he stabs BOY) *TS4*
189 jack-knife!] jack-knife *TS6*
190 there—there—there! *TS4*
Directions after 190 (He stabs again and again and then sings) *TS6[1]* (He stabs again and again. The window goes dark. He sings) *TS6[2]* (he stabs again and again, the window grows dark. (he sings) *TS4*
191 "Hush-a-bye] Hush-a-bye *TS6* knight,] knight *TS6*
192 Thy] They *TS4* lady] lady, *TS6, TS4* bright,"] bright *TS6[1]* bright, *TS6[2]*
194 mother. *TS6*
Directions after 195a The stage *TS6, TS4* light. *TS4*
196 It] That *TS6[1]*
198 mother,] mother *TS6*
200 consequence.] consequence *TS6* consequence; *TS4*
201 lad because of his youth *TS6[1]* lad for he was grown *TS6[2]* lad for he was growing up, *TS6[3]* up,] up *TS4*
202 fancy,] fancy *TS6*
203 Beget, and pass pollution on. *TS6, TS4*
204 wretched, *TS4*
205 harmless. When *TS4*
207 again,] again *TS6*
208 the money *TS6, TS4* dropped, *TS4*
Directions after 210 cleans the knife and] *lacking in TS6[1]*
211 Hoof beats, O my God, hoof beats! *TS6[1]* Hoof beats, dear God, *TS6[2]* God, *TS4*
212 returns, beat, beat; *TS6, TS4*
216 once, *TS6, TS4* times!] times *TS6[1]* times. *TS6[2], TS4*
217 its dream!] its' dream *TS6* its dream. *TS4*
219 dead! *TS4*

Notes on Textual Problems in TSS 5, 6, and 4

Unless otherwise indicated, notes refer to TS5.

The letter ''A'' in the upper right margin is in pencil.

TS6 On every page the letter ''B'' appears in pencil in the upper right margin.

TS6 Directions before l. 1 No bracket encloses directions.

4b The words ''Study that house'' are typed over with ampersands.

12 According to Edward O'Shea, in *A Descriptive Catalog of W. B. Yeats's Library* (New York: Garland Publishing, Inc., 1985), there are five drafts of line 12: ''Having come this way before'' / or / ''You have come etc.'' / or ''So you have been etc.'' / or ''What you have come this way before.'', all of which appear inside the back cover of G. N. M. Tyrrell's *Science and Psychical Phenomena* (1938), which Yeats was reading when he prepared TS5.

15 TS4 The word ''house'' is deleted with typed ampersands and followed by the word ''tree.''

16b The words ''A silly old man'' are deleted with ampersands.

TS4 After 16 ''X to L C'' appears in pencil, possibly in Yeats's hand, to the left of ''A silly old man,'' possibly to indicate ''Crosses to left center.'' This direction, and others like it in TS4, suggest that this typescript might have been used as a rehearsal text.

TS4 After directions before l. 24 ''X up to door'' appears in pencil, perhaps to indicate ''Crosses up to the door,'' possibly in Yeats's hand, to the left of the line, and the word ''sits'' appears in pencil, possibly also in Yeats's hand, to the right of the line.

28 TS4 ''X to OM.'' appears in pencil, possibly in Yeats's hand, to the right of the line possibly to indicate ''Crosses to Old Man.''

42 The words ''(is going)'' in pencil in the right margin were probably intended as the beginning of a new stage direction. They were not transferred to TS7.

43 The words ''Stop,'' ''sit,'' and ''there'' appear to have been written over some letters inscribed in pencil that are illegible; the line ''Stop; sit there upon that stone'' is in a shade of ink distinctly blacker than the shade of blue-black used throughout TS5.

44 The caret, directional line, and the deletion line through l. 44 are in pencil. In TS6, possibly the terminal punctuation was added in holograph after the word ''tree¢'' was typed.

44–45 TS4 ''boy sits'' appears in pencil, probably in Yeats's hand, to the right of these lines.

45 TS6 The indecipherable punctuation at the end of the line has been cancelled and a comma has been added.

53 ''him'' has been deleted in pencil and ''her'' has been added in pencil.

67 TS6 The words ''Some came,'' were typed first, but the typist then deleted ''Some'' with typed ampersands and typed ''Or'' to the left of ''Some.''

78–79 TS4 ''That he might keep me upon his level'' is typed between these lines and has been deleted with typed ampersands.

93 Possibly the caret after ''Fair'' is a period.

95 TS6 The period after ''road'' in $TS6^2$ was changed to a caret in $TS6^3$. After $TS6^3$, Yeats further revised ''roads'' to ''road,'' which he retained in TS5.

112 TS4 A dash and two curved brackets, inscribed in pencil, probably in Mrs. Yeats's or Yeats's hand, enclose the words ''or may do.''

113 TS4 What appears to be the word ''use'' is inscribed in pencil, possibly in Yeats's hand, to the left of the line.

124 This line has been deleted in pencil.

137a Probably after cancelling ''That is now'', Yeats omitted ''now'' after ''And'' and inserted a period at the end of the line. He then inserted ''is'' (which is in ink of a distinctly bluer shade than the shade of blue-black used throughout TS5) after ''that'', and then added ''now'' at the end of the line but forgot to cancel the period after ''chamber.'' This line belongs after line 137.

140–141 TS4 These lines have been deleted in pencil.

142 TS4 ''X to LC'' appears in pencil, possibly in Yeats's hand, to the left of the line.

146 TS4 ''light out—'' appears in pencil, probably in Yeats's hand, to the left of the line.

155–156 TS4 ''X to L C'' appears in pencil, possibly in Yeats's hand, between these lines on the left side of the page.

159 TS4 ''Boy to L'' appears in pencil, possibly in Yeats's hand, to the right of ''Begetting me.''

159 TS4 ''X to boy'' appears in pencil, possibly in Yeats's hand, to the left of the words ''Come back!''

161 ''in'' has been deleted in pencil.

169 In reading the uncorrected typescript, when Yeats reached the end of page 6^r he decided to add some new lines, which he began on page $6i^r$ by copying the *directions* that follow line 174. After writing lines a–c on page $6i^r$, he returned to TS5 in order to transfer the lines on page $6i^r$ to page 6^v. Instead, on page 6^v he began to revise lines that he eventually decided to insert after line 169 on page 6^r, rather than after the direction that follows line 174 as he originally intended to place them when he began to revise. On page 6^v he then added lines a–b and the new directions that follow them. When he reached ''They stand looking at each other,'' he returned to page 6^r and to the new addition on page $6i^r$, and continued to transfer to page 6^v what he had written on that page. But as he transferred to page 6^v the revisions he made on $6i^r$, he introduced fresh changes.

173 TS4 ''X to R'' appears in pencil, possibly in Yeats's hand, to the right of the line.

177 TS5 Possibly the period after ''away'' was changed to a comma or perhaps deleted.

180a Yeats added the caret and the directional line, and the words ''dead, living'' above the line Mrs. Yeats had already transferred to page $7s^{1r}$ (line $180a^{1}$). Yeats himself then transferred his earlier revisions back to page 7^{r}. But when he did, he neglected to insert either thc carets or the comma after the word ''dead.'' He then did cancel the words ''stands there'' on page 7^{r}, but he neglected to cancel them on page $7s^{1}$.

$180a^{1}$ This line was written in ink by Mrs. Yeats.

$185a^{1}$–$185h^{1}$ and $180a^{1}$ represent revisions on a carbon that is identical to TS5, 7^{r}, which is also a carbon.

185a–e Revisions of the cancelled lines 185f–h, which were further revised on page $7s^{1r}$.

$185a^{1}$–c^{1} Revisions of page 7^{r}, lines 185a–e. These lines, inserted by Yeats, are in pencil, although ''Horrible Horrible'' above line $185b^{1}$ is probably in ink and probably line $185c^{1}$ has been deleted in ink. The caret and directional line are probably in pencil.

$185d^{1}$–h^{1} Lines Mrs. Yeats transferred from page 7^{r}, lines 185b–e, and in the process introduced the following changes: the exclamation mark in line d^{1}; the upper case G and the apostrophe in line g^{1}; the exclamation mark in line h^{1}; and the period in the direction following line h^{1}. The lines are probably in ink but were then deleted, probably by Yeats, probably in pencil.

Directions after 190 ''he sig'' has been typed over with ampersands in the right margin.

186 The original terminal punctuation is treated in the variants as a period, although it is possibly a semicolon; the typed punctuation was further revised in the hand either of Yeats or Mrs. Yeats to what appears to be a comma. It is treated as a comma in the variants.

210 Possibly the period after ''men'' is a holograph addition.

213 Possibly the period after ''dream'' is a holograph addition.

Evolution of the Text from TS5 to the Printed Versions

After having revised TS5 and added the new lines on pages 6^v and 7, Yeats turned to a clean carbon of TS5, which was to become TS7. Pages 1, 2, 3, 4, and 5 of TS7 contain holograph additions, all of which Yeats and Mrs. Yeats transferred from Yeats's holograph additions on TS5. There is a variant in punctuation in the one line Yeats himself transferred and also in a few of those Mrs. Yeats transferred. Since this was to be the final typescript of *Purgatory,* the pagination on the clean carbon of TS5 was adjusted to the pagination of the *On the Boiler* typescript to which TS7 would be appended. The numbers 1, 2, 3, 4, and 5 in the upper right margin were replaced with holograph inscriptions of the numbers 52, 53, 54, 55, and 56. When Yeats came to page 6 of TS5, however, he did not use the carbon of that page for the new TS7. Instead the holograph additions on page 6^v, to be inserted after line 169, were typed on a new page and, following the new pagination, that page bears the number 57 in the upper right margin. This page, and pages 58 and 59, which are also new pages, incorporate the revisions Yeats made on the verso of page 6^v and those he made on page $7s^1$ of TS5. Although the words on pages 58 and 59 and on pages 7 and 8 of TS5 are spaced differently, the only variant wording occurs on TS5, 7: the stage directions following line 190 end with the words "*he sings.*" These are omitted on TS7, 58. We might suppose that if Yeats had wanted to retain them, he would have added them to the new typescript. TS7, then, incorporates those revisions and additions Yeats made on TS5. Although some holograph additions on TS7 are in Mrs. Yeats's hand, the lines she transferred from TS5 were those Yeats himself had inscribed there. It is impossible to know with certainty whether Yeats actually instructed Mrs. Yeats to make the few changes in punctuation she introduced, or whether she made them without his instructions, although it is clear that those she made remained on the page proofs with his approval (see page 154).

It is possible that this typescript was the one that Yeats gave to F. R. Higgins at the end of June and that Higgins, probably early in July, gave to the Longford printer, although it is more likely that it was a duplicate of TS7 which the printer actually used and which is now lost. The galleys Longford prepared from TS7 were sent to Yeats some time in the autumn, when he corrected and returned them to the printer. From Yeats's corrected galleys, which he never again saw and which are now lost, the Longford printer then prepared page proofs. When the Longford firm sent the new set of page proofs to Yeats in late December or early January, the printer did not send with them (or if they were sent they did not reach Yeats) the corrected galleys against which Yeats could read the page proofs. He corrected the first set of page proofs, nevertheless, without his corrected galleys to guide him, and returned them to the printer knowing that he might have made revisions on the galleys that he did not make on the page proofs—and vice versa. In order to avoid a similar problem with the corrected page proofs, he asked the printer to prepare a new set of page proofs from those he had corrected, and to return to him his corrected proofs with the newly prepared second set. Longford then prepared a second set from the page proofs Yeats corrected. The few discrepancies that occur between the first and second set were probably due to Longford's efforts to incorporate revisions Yeats had made on the now lost galleys but which he did not incorporate into the first set of corrected page proofs, although about this we cannot be certain. If the printer had returned the first set of Yeats's corrected galleys, or if they had survived, these or possibly the page proofs set from them and on which Yeats made further corrections would supercede TS7 (or a possible duplicate) as the preferred reading text. But since Yeats corrected the Longford proofs without the galleys to guide him, and since the galleys have not survived, I have chosen to key the variants in the readings that follow to the typescript rather than to the first set of Longford page proofs, even though this is the last version of the play Yeats saw and on which he made corrections. The second set, which was returned after his death, was corrected in ink and pencil by Mrs. Yeats and one or more unidentified hands. The Longford edition of *On the Boiler* was prepared from this set, but Mrs. Yeats, who was unhappy with the edition, had nearly all of the five hundred copies that were printed destroyed—all but four, according to Wade. She then commissioned the Alex. Thom Company to print a new edition. In the Scribner archive at the University of Texas at Austin are two posthumously prepared printings of *Purgatory,* one of which is a copy of this edition. At some stage of preparation Scribner severed the pages of the play from those of the essay, "On the Boiler," for the purposes of printing them in separate volumes for the edition of Yeats's work they had planned but which they eventually abandoned. The other is of page proofs printed on paper of the same quality and stock as that used for the Cuala edition of *Last Poems and Two Plays* and is marked "1st proofs. *revise,*" which is cancelled, and "corrected," which is not cancelled. These probably represent an intermediary stage of preparation for the version Cuala eventually printed and whose variants are provided below (pages 191–99). The corrections, in an unidentified hand, to move half lines several spaces to the right, and a few holograph corrections of typographical errors, were carried out by the printer. There are, however, five discrepancies in punctuation, probably attributable to the fact that other corrections, including new pagination, were made on a duplicate set of proofs from which a new set was prepared for the edition Cuala finally produced. In addition to having different pagination, the page proofs have "April 1938" inscribed after the last line of the play and "THE CURTAIN FALLS" follows the last line of the play in the Cuala edition but is lacking on the proofs. Most likely, these discarded proofs found their way into the archive when, after Yeats's death, additional materials were sent, probably by Mrs. Yeats, to supplement those Yeats himself had already deposited with Scribner's for their projected edition of his work. The severed pages of *On the Boiler* suggest that Scribner had decided to use the Alex. Thom printing rather than the corrected proofs, which had been superceded by another set that did not find its way to Scribner's. The proofs, which neither Scribner nor any other press published, are as remote from Yeats's authorial decisions as later posthumous versions whose significance is necessarily negligible for the purposes of evolving a reading text.

When the printed texts differ from TS7 and from the first set of page proofs prepared for the Longford edition, variants in the second set of page proofs and in all subsequent printed editions of the play were introduced by Mrs. Yeats, F. R. Higgins, or Thomas Mark, who served as editor at Macmillan, on all of whom Yeats frequently relied for advice (although he did not always follow it).

In the collations that follow, TS7 in its final form is used as the basic reading text. Mechanical errors have been corrected silently as, for example, in such typeovers as "y" over "t" in the word "Study" in line 4 and in such letters as the "a" which has been deleted in pencil, following the word "Looked" in line 51. Errors involving the spacing of words have been regularized as, for example, in line 20 where "Before" has been moved one space to the left to rectify the margin, and in line 22 where two rather than three spaces have been left before "life." and "Stand." Spacing has also been corrected where words have been inadvertently run together as in "outall" in line 210. Letters that have been inadvertently omitted from words as, for example, "l" between "u" and "d" in the word "should" in line 143 have been supplied. Other corrections, however, such as the conversion of the word "I" to "If" in line 151 are recorded in *Notes on Textual Problems in TS7 and the Printed Versions*. Round and square brackets have been preserved, but underscored words in the typescripts have been italicized. In the first set of Longford page proofs all stage directions are in roman rather than italic print, but Yeats's revisions of them throughout, excepting those after "PURGATORY," lines 23, 191, and 198, which were probably inadvertently overlooked, call for italics. The revised readings are uniformly given below. Other significant revisions that Yeats called for on the first set of Longford page proofs are recorded in the variants and, where appropriate, are treated separately in *Notes on Textual Problems in TS7 and the Printed Versions*. Yeats's instructions to the printer, such as "Same type as rest," which appears in the top left margin, and "Same print as heading on page 30," which appears in the top right margin of the title page, are not transcribed, nor are those that are inscribed on page 34, instructions that call for uniform spacing and the adjustment of the left margin. He repeated these instructions on page 39, referring the printer to page 34, and inscribed his initials below the entry. These inscriptions can be readily observed in the photographic reproductions of the page proofs.

In the second set of Longford page proofs all stage directions, which are in italics, are enclosed in round brackets. Revisions throughout, in an unidentified hand, call for the deletion of both round brackets and the substitution of a square for round left bracket, with the exception of those after the title, and the direction "(Staring at window)" after line 170, the revisions of which were probably inadvertently overlooked. The revised readings are uniformly given below. Other revisions Mrs. Yeats called for on the second set of Longford page proofs are recorded, including those that restore the text to conform on Textual Problems in TS7. Where the reading of the second set of Longford page proofs before revisions is identical to that of TS7, as, for example, in line 76, the reading of the second set of Longford page proofs is not given. And where the second set of Longford page proofs is not revised, there is no entry for the revised set of Longford page proofs. Where appropriate, special problems are treated in *Notes on Textual Problems in TS7 and the Printed Versions*. Words in TS7 to which variants are keyed are enclosed in the right brackets only where punctuation is dropped, or where words in lines to which variants are keyed are not readily identifiable. In all other instances, where punctuation differs, the variants follow the number of the lines in which the word or words appear, and to which they are keyed.

TS5	TS5 revised to its final version.
LPP1	The first set of Longford page proofs with Yeats's corrections.
LPP2	The second set of uncorrected Longford page proofs, which incorporates Yeats's revisions on LPP1.
$LPP2^1$	Proof revisions on LPP2.
LE	The Longford Edition.
A	The Alex. Thom Edition, *On the Boiler* (Dublin: Cuala, 1939).
L	*Last Poems and Two Plays by William Butler Yeats* (Dublin: Cuala, 1939).

PURGATORY

		(A ruined house and a bare tree in the background.)
1	Boy:	Half door, hall door
2		Hither and thither day and night
3		Hill or hollow, shouldering this pack.
4		Hearing you talk.
	Old Man:	Study that house.
5		I think about its jokes and stories;
6		I try to remember what the butler
7		Said to a drunken gamekeeper
8		In mid-October, but I cannot,
9		I cannot, and none living can.
10		Where are the jokes and stories of a house,
11		Its threshold gone to patch a pig-stye?
12	Boy:	So you have come this path before?
13	Old Man:	The moonlight falls upon the path,
14		The shadow of a cloud upon the house
15		And that symbolical; study that tree,
16		What is it like?
	Boy:	A silly old man.
17	Old Man:	It's like—no matter what it's like.
18		I saw it a year ago stripped bare as now,
19		I saw it fifty years ago

Above PURGATORY April 1938. *LPP2*, deleted in *LPP2[1]*

Directions after PURGATORY (A] [A *LPP2[1]* background.)] background). *LPP1* background). *LPP2, LE, A,* background. *LPP2[1]*

1 Half door, *A* hall door, *LPP2[1]*

2 thither, *TS5* night, *TS5, LPP2[1]*

3 pack.] pack *TS5, LPP2, A* pack, *LPP2[1]*

4 house.] house *A*

7 a] a *revised to* an old *then restored with* stet *LPP1*

8 cannot. *LPP2[1]*

9 If I cannot, none living can. *LPP1, LPP2, LE, A, L*

10 house,] house *L*

11 pig-sty? *A, L*

14 house, *LPP2[1]*

15 that] that's *LPP1, LPP2, LE, A, L*

16 A] 'A' *revised to* A *LPP1*

After 18 So I chose a better trade *LPP2* So I chose a better trade. *LPP2[1], A* So I chose a better trade *LE*

20 Before the thunder-bolt had riven it,
21 Green leaves, ripe leaves, leaves thick as butter,
22 Fat, greasy life. Stand there and look,
23 Because there is somebody in that house.
(*The BOY puts down pack and stands in the doorway*)
24 Boy: There's nobody here.
Old Man: There's somebody there.
25 Boy: The floor is gone, the windows gone,
26 And where there should be roof there's sky,
27 And here's a bit of an egg-shell thrown
28 Out of a jackdaw's nest.
Old Man: But there are some
29 That do not care what's gone, what's left,
30 The souls in Purgatory that come back
31 To habitations and familiar spots.
32 Boy: Your wits are out again.
Old Man: Re-live
33 Their transgressions, and that not once
34 But many times, they know at last
35 The consequence of those transgressions
36 Whether upon others or upon themselves;
37 If upon others, others may bring help
38 For when the consequence is at an end
39 The dream must end; if upon themselves
40 There is no help but in themselves
41 And in the mercy of God.
Boy: I have had enough!
42 Talk to the jackdaws, if talk you must.
43 Old Man: Stop! Sit there upon that stone—
44 That is the house where I was born.
45 Boy: The big old house that was burnt down?
46 Old Man: My mother that was your grand-dam owned it,

---

20 thunderbolt *A*
Directions after 23 (The BOY . . . doorway)] (The BOY . . . doorway) *LPP1* [The BOY . . . doorway *LPP2[1]* (The BOY . . . doorway). *LE, A* (The boy . . . doorway) *L*
29 gone,] gone *LPP1, LPP2, revised to* gone, *LPP2[1]* left,] left; *LPP2[1], LE, A, L* left: *LPP2[1] further revised*
34 times; *A*
36 others, *LPP1, LPP2, LE, L*
37 If upon] Upon *LPP1, LPP2, LE, A, L* help, *LPP2[1], LE, A*
38 is] it *revised to* is *LPP1*
39 if upon themselves] upon themselves *revised to* upon themselves, *LPP1* upon themselves, *LPP2, LE, A* upon themselves *L*
41 God.] God *L*
43 Stop!] Stop; *TS5* Stop. *LPP2* Stop! *LPP2[1]* stone—] stone *TS5* stone. *LPP1, LPP2, LE, A, L*
45 big old house] big house *LPP2* big old house *LPP2[1]*

47 This scenery and this countryside,
48 Kennel and stable, horse and hound—
49 She had a horse at the Curragh, and there met
50 My father, a groom in a training stable;
51 Looked at him and married him.
52 Her mother never spoke to her again,
53 And she did right.
Boy: What's right and wrong?
54 My grand-dad got the girl and the money.
55 Old Man: Looked at him and married him,
56 And he squandered everything she had.
57 She never knew the worst, because
58 She died in giving birth to me,
59 But now she knows it all, being dead.
60 Great people lived and died in this house;
61 Magistrates, colonels, members of Parliament,
62 Captains and governors, and long ago
63 Men that had fought at Aughrim and the Boyne.
64 Some that had gone on government work
65 To London or to India came home to die,
66 Or came from London every spring
67 To look at the May-blossom in the park.
68 They had loved the trees that he cut down
69 To pay what he had lost at cards
70 Or spent on horses, drink and women;
71 Had loved the house, had loved all
72 The intricate passages of the house,
73 But he killed the house; to kill a house
74 Where great men grew up, married, died,
75 I here declare a capital offence.
76 Boy: My God, but you had luck. Grand clothes,
77 And maybe a grand horse to ride.
78 Old Man: That he might keep me upon his level
79 He never sent me to school, but some
80 Half-loved me for my half of her,

---

50 stable, *LPP2[1]*, *L*
61 Parliament,] Parliament *LPP2* Parliament, *LPP2[1]*
62 Governors, *LPP1*, *LPP2*, *LE*, *A*, *L*
64 Government *LPP2[1]*
65 India, *L*
67 may-blossom *LPP2[1]*
73 house;] house: *LE*
76 luck! *LPP2[1]*, *A*
80 her; *LPP2[1]*, her: *A*

81		A gamekeeper's wife taught me to read,
82		A Catholic curate taught me Latin.
83		There were old books and books made fine
84		By eighteenth century French binding, books
85		Modern and ancient, books by the ton.
86	Boy:	What education have you given me?
87	Old Man:	I gave the education that befits
88		A bastard that a peddlar got
89		Upon a tinker's daughter in a ditch.
90		When I had come into my sixteenth year
91		My father burned down the house when drunk.
92	Boy:	But that is my age, sixteen years old.
93		At the Puck Fair
93	Old Man:	And everything was burnt;
94		Books, library, all were burnt.
95	Boy:	Is what I have heard upon the road the truth,
96		That you killed him in the burning house?
97	Old Man:	There's nobody here but our two selves?
98	Boy:	Nobody, Father.
	Old Man:	I stuck him with a knife,
99		That knife that cuts my dinner now,
100		And after that I left him in the fire;
101		They dragged him out, somebody saw
102		The knife-wound but could not be certain
103		Because the body was all black and charred.
104		Then some that were his drunken friends
105		Swore they would put me upon trial,
106		Spoke of quarrels, a threat I had made.
107		The gamekeeper gave me some old clothes,
108		I ran away, worked here and there
109		Till I became a pedlar on the roads,
110		No good trade, but good enough
111		Because I am my father's son,
112		Because of what I did or may do.
113		Listen to the hoof beats! Listen, listen!
114	Boy:	I cannot hear a sound.
	Old Man:	Beat! Beat!

84 eighteenth-century *LPP2*[1]
88 pedlar *LPP2*[1], *A*, *L*
90 come to sixteen years old *LPP1*, *LPP2*, *LE*, *A*, *L*
92 old.] old *TS5*, *A* old, *LPP2*[1]
93 Fair. *LPP1*, *LPP2*, *LE*, *A*, *L*
100 fire. *LPP2*[1]
113 Listen, Listen! *L* hoof-beats! *LPP2*[1]

115 This night is the anniversary
116 Of my mother's wedding night,
117 Or of the night wherein I was begotten.
118 My father is riding from the public house
119 A whiskey bottle under his arm.
(*a window is lit, showing a young girl*)
120 Look at the window; she stands there
121 Listening, the servants are all in bed,
122 She is alone, he has stayed late
123 Bragging and drinking in the public house.
124 Boy: There's nothing but an empty gap in the wall.
125 You have made it up. No, you are mad!
126 You are getting madder every day.
127 Old Man: It's louder now because he rides
128 Upon a gravelled avenue
129 All grass today. The hoof beat stops,
130 He has gone to the other side of the house
131 Gone to the stable, put the horse up.
132 She has gone down to open the door.
133 This night she is no better than her man
134 And does not mind that he is half drunk,
135 She is mad about him. They mount the stairs
136 She brings him into her own chamber.
137 And that is the marriage chamber now.
138 The window is dimly lit again
139 O do not let him touch you! It is not true
140 That drunken men cannot beget
141 And if he touch he must beget
142 And you must bear his murderer.

---

118 public house *LPP2* public-house, *LPP2*[1]
119 whiskey-bottle *LPP2*
Directions after 119 (a window is lit,] (a window is lit *LPP1 but* (A window is lit *LPP1 revised, LE, A, L* (A window is lit *LPP2* [A window is lit *LPP2*[1] girl)] girl. *LPP2*[1] girl). *A*
123 public-house. *LPP2*[1] publichouse. *A*
124 wall.] wall *TS5*
129 to-day. *LPP1, LPP2, LE, A, L* hoop beat *revised to* hoof beat *LPP1*, hoof-beat *LPP2*[1]
130 house, *LPP2*[1], *L*
131 To put the horse up. All that is hidden *TS5*
After 131 but I can see it all in the mind. *TS5*
134 drunk. *LPP2*
136 brings] brings brings *revised to* brings *LPP1*
137 marriage chamber. now *TS5* marriage-chamber now. *LPP2*[1]
138 again. *LPP1, LPP2, LE, A, L*
After 138 And the passage door is open; now / That door is shut and the window dark. *TS5*
139 O do] Do *LPP1, LPP2, LE, A, L*
140 beget, *LPP2*[1]

143 Deaf! Both deaf! If I should throw
144 A stick or a stone they would not hear;
145 And that's a proof my wits are out.
146 But here's a problem: she must live
147 Through everything in exact detail,
148 Driven to it by remorse, and yet
149 Can she renew the sexual act
150 And find no pleasure in it, and if not
151 If pleasure and remorse must both be there
152 Which is the greater?
I lack schooling.
153 Go fetch Tertullian; he and I
154 Will ravel all that problem out
155 Whilst those two lie upon the mattress
156 Begetting me.
Come back! Come back!
157 And so you thought to slip away,
158 My bag of money between your fingers,
159 And that I could not talk and see!
160 You have been rummaging in the pack.
(*The light in the window has faded out*)
161 Boy: You never gave me a share.
162 Old Man: And had I given it, young as you are
163 You would have spent it upon drink.
164 Boy: What if I did? I had a right
165 To get my share and spend it as I chose.
166 Old Man: Give me that bag and no more words.
167 Boy: I will not.
Old Man: I can change that song.
(*They struggle for the bag. In the struggle it drops, scattering the money. The old man staggers but does not fall. They stand looking at each other*)

---

144 a stone] stone *L*
146 here's] there's *LPP1, LPP2, LE, A, L*
150 not, *LPP2*[1], *LE, A, L*
151 there, *LPP2*[1]
156 Come back! came back! *TS5*
Directions after 160 out). *A*
161 You kept it all and never gave me a share. *TS5* You never gave me my right share. *LPP1, LPP2, LE, A, L*
162 are. *LPP2* are, *LPP2*[1]
165 my share] it *LPP1, LPP2, LE, A, L*
167 I will not.] No. *TS5* I can change that song.] I will break your fingers. *LPP1, LPP2, LE, A, L*
Directions after 167 (They] They *TS5* [They *LPP2*[1] They *L* In the struggle it drops, scattering the money.] The boy drops it *TS5* old man] Old Man *TS5, LPP2*[1] OLD MAN *A* staggers] staggers back *TS5* each] tach *LPP1 but* each *LPP1 revised* other)] other. *A* other.) *L*

168 Boy: What if I killed you? You killed my grand-dad.
169 Because you were young and he was old.
170 Now I am young and you are old.
(*window is lit up, a man is seen pouring whiskey into a glass.*)
Old Man: (*staring at window*)
171 Better looking, those sixteen years—
172 Boy: What are you muttering?
Old Man: Younger—and yet
173 She should have known he was not her kind.
174 Boy: What are you saying? Out with it!
(*Old Man points to window.*)
175 Boy: My God! The window is lit up
176 And somebody stands there, although
177 The floorboards are all burnt away.
178 Old Man: The window is lit up because my father
179 Has come to find a glass for his whiskey.
180 He leans there like some tired beast.
181 Boy: A dead, living, murdered man.
182 Old Man: Then the bride sleep fell upon Adam;
183 Where did I read those words?
And yet
184 There's nothing leaning in the window
185 But the impression upon my mother's mind,
186 Being dead she is alone in her remorse.
187 Boy: A body that was a bundle of old bones
188 Before I was born. Horrible! Horrible!
(*he covers his eyes*)

---

168 killed you?] kill you. *TS5* grand-dad.] grand dad *TS5* grand-dad *LPP2, L* grand-dad, *LPP2*[1], *A*
169 old; *A*
Directions after 170 (window is] (Window is *LPP2, LE, A* The window is *LPP2*[1] (A window is *L* up, a man] up. Man *TS5* glass.)] glass) *TS5, LPP2, LE, A* (staring at window)] *lacking in TS5* (Staring at window) *LPP2, LE, A, L* (staring at window) *LPP2*[1]
171 Better-looking, *LPP2*[1]
172 muttering?] muttering *TS5*
173 kind.] kind *TS5*
174 saying—out with it *TS5*
Directions after 174 (Old Man] Old Man *TS5* [Old Man *LPP2*[1] (OLD MAN *A* window.)] window *TS5* window. *LPP2*[1] window). *A* window) *L*
175 God! The] God the *L* window] winow *TS5*
181 A dead living murdered buried man *TS5*
182 'Then *LPP2*[1] bride-sleep *LPP2*[1], *A* Adam;] Adam: *LPP1, LPP2, LE, A, L* Adam': *LPP2*[1]
After 187 That was a bundle of old bones / Before I was born—O my god / Horrible, horrible horrible. *TS5*
Directions after 188 (he] He *TS5* (he *LPP1 but* (He *LPP1 revised, LE, A, L* [He *LPP2*[1] eyes)] eyes. *LPP1, LPP2*[1] eyes.) *LE, A*

189 Old Man: That beast there would know nothing, being nothing,
190 If I should kill a man under the window,
191 He would not even turn his head.
(*he stabs the BOY*)
192 My father and my son on the same jack-knife!
193 That finishes—there—there—there—
(*he stabs again and again. The window grows dark.*)
194 Old Man: "Hush-a-bye baby, thy father's a knight,
195 Thy mother a lady, lovely and bright."
196 No, that is something that I read in a book
197 And if I sing it must be to my mother,
198 And I lack rhyme.
(*the stage has grown dark except where the tree stands in white light*)
Study that tree.
199 It stands there like a purified soul,
200 All cold, sweet, glistening light.
201 Dear mother, the window is dark again
202 But you are in the light because
203 I finished all that consequence.
204 I killed that lad for he was growing up,
205 He would soon take some woman's fancy,
206 Beget, and pass pollution on.
207 I am a wretched foul old man
208 And therefore harmless when I have stuck

---

189 nothing, being nothing,] nothing, being *revised to add* ded *but then entire line deleted, underlined for "stet" and revised further to add* nothing *LPP1* nothing being nothing. *L*

190 window; *TS5* window. *LPP1, LPP2, LE*

Directions after 191 (he] (he *LPP1 but* (He *LPP1 revised* [He *LPP2*^{1} (He *LE, A, L* BOY)] BOY) *LPP1* BOY. *LPP2*^{1} BOY). *A* boy) *L*

Directions after 193 (he] (he *LPP1 but* (He *LPP1 revised* (He *LE, A, L* [He *LPP2*^{1} dark.)] dark. he sings) *TS5* dark) *LPP2* dark *LPP2*^{1} dark) *LE* dark). *A*

194 *line repeated LPP2 second occurrence deleted LPP2*^{1}

195 bright," *TS5*

196 book, *LPP2*^{1}*, A*

197 sing, *A*

Directions after 198 (the stage] (the stage *LPP1 but* (The stage *LPP1 revised* [The stage *LPP2*^{1} (The stage *LE, A, L* except] *except LPP2 except LPP2*^{1} light)] light). *LPP1* light). *LPP2, LE, A* light. *LPP2*^{1} light.) *L*

201 again, *LPP2*^{1}

204 for he was growing up,] *revised to* because he had grown up *LPP1* because he had grown up, *LPP2, LE, A possibly revised to* had he *LPP2*^{1}

205 soon take some woman's fancy,] *revised to* have struck a woman s fancy *then revised further to* have taken a woman s fancy *then revised further to* have struck a woman s fancy *LPP1* have struck a woman's fancy, *LPP2, LE, A*

206 Beget,] *revised to* Begot, *LPP1* Begot, *LPP2, LE, A* Beget *L* pass] *revised to* passed *LPP1* passed *LPP2, LE, A* polution *TS5*

208 harmless. When *LPP1, LPP2, LE, A, L*

209 This old jack knife into a sod
210 And pulled it out all bright again,
211 And picked up all the money that he dropped
212 I'll to a distant place, and there
213 Tell my old jokes among new men.
(*he cleans the knife and begins to pick up money*)
214 Hoof beats! Dear God
215 How quickly it returns—beat—beat—
216 Her mind cannot hold up that dream.
217 Twice a murderer and all for nothing,
218 And she must animate that dead night
219 Not once but many times!
O God!
220 Release my mother's soul from its dream!
221 Mankind can do no more. Appease
222 The misery of the living and the remorse of
the dead.

---

209 jack-knife *TS5, LPP2[1], A, L*
211 the] th *TS5*
Directions after 213 (he] (He *TS5* (he *LPP1 but* (He *LPP1 revised, LE, A, L* [He *LPP2[1]* money)] money *LPP2[1]* money). *A* money.) *L*
214 Hoof beats!] Hoof-beats! *LPP2[1]* God] God, *LPP2[1]*
215 beat—beat—] beat—beat—! *LPP2[1]*
219 God!] God *LPP1, LPP2, LE, A* God, *LPP2[1]*
After last line April 1938 *LPP2[1]* April, 1938. *LE, A*
After date ? Curtain *LPP2[1]* THE CURTAIN FALLS *L*

Notes on Textual Problems in TS7 and the Printed Versions

Unless otherwise indicated, notes refer to TS7. Also, unless otherwise indicated all holograph additions on TS7 are in black ink and were transferred by Mrs. Yeats from Yeats's holograph additions on TS5.

The number 52 in the upper right margin was added by Yeats and follows the pagination of the typescript of *On the Boiler*.

3 Period added by Mrs. Yeats.

12 The typed words ''What do you know about this place'' but not the punctuation have been deleted. Yeats transferred the words ''So you have come this path before,'' which appear in his hand above the line, from TS5, where they are also inscribed in his hand above the same deleted line.

After 18 ''So I chose a better trade'', l. 11 of the poem ''The Statesman's Holiday,'' printed on the preceding page of *On the Boiler* proofs to which *LPP1* and *LPP2* were joined. The line appears neither on any of the typescripts nor on Yeats's corrected page proofs. It is probable that in preparing the second set of page proofs the Longford printer consulted not only the first page proofs Yeats corrected and returned but also the now lost corrected galleys. Mrs. Yeats retained the line on LPP2 which was printed in the Longford Edition and the Alex. Thom Edition, but dropped in *Last Poems and Two Plays*.

43 In transferring this line from TS5 to TS7, Mrs. Yeats substituted an exclamation mark for a semicolon in TS5 after the word ''stop.'' Mrs. Yeats's indecipherable punctuation after the word ''stone'' is probably a dash or possibly an exclamation mark, one or the other of which might have been changed from a period; it is treated as a dash in the variants.

52 The word ''him'' has been cancelled and the word ''her'' added in pencil. The page number 3 is cancelled and 54 added in pencil by Yeats. The page number 4 is cancelled and 55 added in pencil by Yeats.

90 Mrs. Yeats cancelled the words ''reached my fifteenth'' and replaced them with ''come into my sixteenth'' as they appear on TS5 in Yeats's hand.

92 ''And'' before ''that'' has been cancelled, a caret has been added, and the word ''But'' has been added; the ''i'' has been inserted before the ''s'' and the comma has been added after the word ''age''; the words ''sixteen years old'' have been transferred from TS5, but the punctuation has been added.

93 "At the Puck Fair" and the word "And" before "everything" have been added; the uppercase "E" has been changed to a lowercase "e" to conform to TS5. The page number 5 is cancelled and 56 has been added in pencil.

124 The words "in the window, all there is black" and the comma have been cancelled and replaced with "but an empty gap in the wall." to conform to TS5, but Mrs. Yeats added the period at the end of the line.

130 The word "To" before "put" is cancelled, a caret has been added, and the words "Gone to the stable" followed by a comma have been added by Yeats in the left margin. The second half of the line: "All that is hidden" has been cancelled by Yeats.

After 131 The line "But I can see it all in the mind" has been cancelled by Yeats.

After 133 Three lines have been cancelled by Mrs. Yeats to conform to TS5.

136 "Now" after the word "chamber" has been cancelled either by Yeats or by Mrs. Yeats to conform to TS5.

137 When Mrs. Yeats transferred to TS7 Yeats's holograph addition of the same line in TS5, "And that is the marriage chamber. now," she omitted the period after the word "chamber," punctuation on TS5 Yeats had neglected to cancel and reposition to follow the word "now."

143 The inadvertent omission of the letter "l" in the word "should" has been emended in the transcription.

151 The inadvertent omission of the letter "f" after the letter "I" has been emended in the transcription.

161 "You never gave me a share", as it appears in TS7, was probably revised by Yeats on the galleys to "You never gave me my right share," was not further revised by him on LPP1, and was retained as it appears there in all of the printed editions.

165 "To get my share and spend it as I chose", as it appears in TS7, was probably revised by Yeats on the galleys to "To get it and spend it as I chose," probably to preserve the four-beat line, was not further revised by him on LPP1, and was retained as it appears there in all of the printed editions.

167 The cancelled word "No" and the exclamation mark that follows it before the words "I will" conform to Yeats's holograph additions on TS5 6^v, but the punctuation was added in the typing of TS7. The word is cancelled and replaced in Yeats's hand with the line he had cancelled in TS5. The words "I can change that song" were probably revised by Yeats on the galleys to "I will break your fingers" as they appear on LPP1 and in all subsequent printed editions.

Directions after 167 The words "(The window is lit, a man is seen pouring whiskey into a glass," which appear after line 170 on LPP1 but after line 167 on LPP2, probably were repositioned by mistake by the printer but retained in that position by Mrs. Yeats. They appear after line 167 in the Longford Edition and in *A* and they appear after line 170 in *Last Poems and Two Plays,* as they do in LPP1, but in *Last Poems and Two Plays* the word "A," instead of the word "The" appears before the word "window." The words "Staring at window" appear after line 170 in LPP2, although they appear as the last direction in LPP1 after line 167. They, too, probably were repositioned by mistake by the printer but were retained in that position by Mrs. Yeats. In *Last Poems and Two Plays* they appear as in LPP1.

Lines 167–174 and the directions that follow 174 have been transferred from Yeats's holograph additions (169a–k) on TS5.

Directions after 170 the word ''seening'' is an uncorrected typographical error which has been corrected to ''seen.'' The words ''(staring at window)'' do not appear on TS5 6v; they were probably inserted by Yeats as TS7 was being prepared.

171 Yeats cancelled the word ''through,'' added a caret, and wrote the word ''those'' above the line.

173 The space between the words ''not'' and ''her'' was filled with the word ''not'' and has been cancelled either by Yeats or by Mrs. Yeats.

181 The period after the word ''man'' was probably added by Yeats, who also probably cancelled the words ''stands there'' after the period. He neglected to cancel the exclamation mark at the end of the line.

182 There appears to be an indecipherable mark through the semi-colon in TS7.

189 In LPP1, either Yeats or Mrs. Yeats deleted the printed line, inscribed ''ded'' in the right margin, underlined the printed words, and probably intended to write ''stet'' in the margin. The word ''nothing'' inscribed in the right margin, which is in Mrs. Yeats's hand, is neither deleted nor underlined.

205 In LPP1, the order of revision is conjectural.

Note: After I prepared this edition I learned of a duplicate set of LPP1, recently acquired by the National Library of Ireland from Michael Yeats's collection, which contains what appear to be markings in the hands of Yeats and Mrs. Yeats, but all of which copy the markings on the set that is reproduced here. In Yeats's one holograph entry on the first page of the play he wrote of the speaker tags: ''Should not be crossed out but put in italics / WBY.'' Two additional differences from LPP1 appear: in the directions after l. 167 ''each'' is not corrected, and in the directions after l. 170 the word ''window'' is marked for an upper case ''W.'' The date, ''April, 1938,'' which appears in print at the head of the page and which is cancelled and moved to the foot of the last page, was probably intended by Yeats to be printed on the preceding page as the date of ''The Statesman's Holiday.''

Appendix

Photographic Reproductions of TS7 and
First Set of the Longford Page Proofs

52

PURGATORY

(A ruined house and a bare trees in the background.)

BOY Half door, hall door
Hither and thither day and night
~~Holding up this old pack~~ Hill or hollow, shouldering this pack.
Hearing you talk.

OLD MAN ~~@@@@@@@@@@@@@@@@@@~~ Study that house.
I think about its jokes and stories;
I try to remember what the butler
Said to a drunken gamekeeper
In mid-October, but I cannot,
I cannot, and none living can.
Where are the jokes and stories of a house ,
Its threshold gone to patch a pig-stye?

BOY ~~What do you know about this place~~ So you have come this path before?

OLD MAN The moonlight falls upon the path,
The shadow of a cloud upon the house
And that symbolical; study that tree,
What is it like?

BOY ~~@@@@@@@@@@@@@@@@@~~A silly old man.

OLD MAN It's like - not matter what it's like.
I saw it a year ago stripped bare as now,
I saw it fifty years ago
Before the thunder-bolt had riven it,
Green leaves, ripe leaves, leaves thick as butter,
Fat, greasy life. Stand there and look,
Because there is somebody in that house.

(The BOY puts down pack and stands in the doorway)

BOY There's nobody here.

OLD MAN There's somebody there.

253

BOY The floor is gone, the windows gone,
And where there should be roof there's sky,
And here's a bit of an egg-shell thrown
Out of a jackdaw's nest.

OLD MAN But there are some
That do not care what's gone, what's left,
The souls in Purgatory that come back
To habitations and familiar spots.

BOY Your wits are out again.

OLD MAN Re-live
Their transgressions, and that not once
But many times, they know at last
The consequence of those transgressions
Whether upon others or upon themselves;
If upon others, others may bring help
For when the consequence is at an end
The dream must end; if upon themselves
There is no help but in themselves
And in the mercy of God.

BOY I have had enough!
Talk to the jackdaws, if talk you must.

OLD MAN Stop! Sit there upon that stone.
~~Sit down upon this stone and~~
~~Wild cut a stick out of that tree.~~

That is the house where I was born.

BOY The big old house that was burnt down?

OLD MAN My mother that was your grand-dam owned it,
This scenery and this countryside,
Kennel and stable, horse and hound -

She had a horse at the Curragh, and there met
My father, a groom in a training stable;
Looked at him and married him.
Her mother never spoke to ~~him~~ her again,
And she did right.

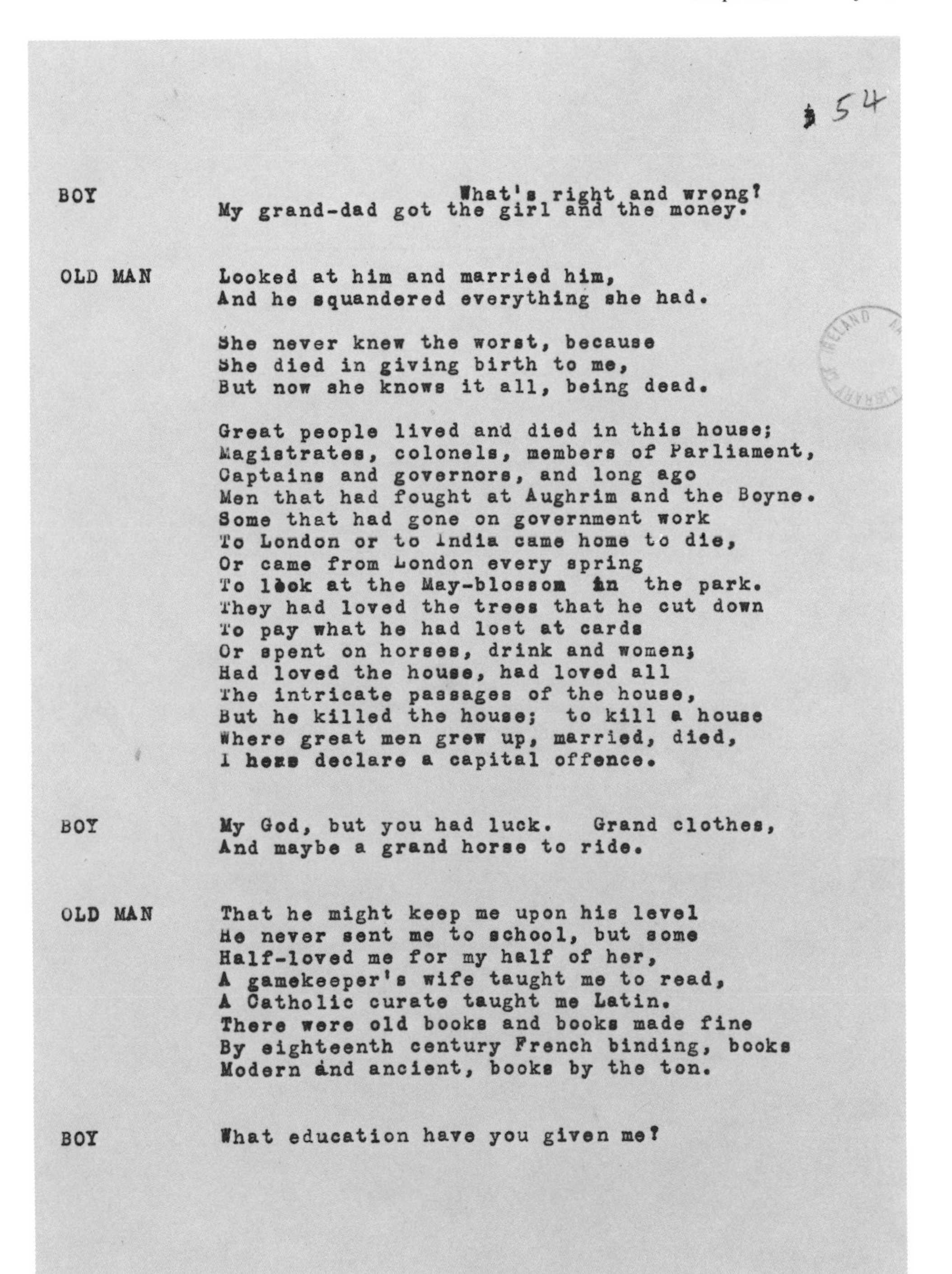

$ 54

BOY What's right and wrong?
My grand-dad got the girl and the money.

OLD MAN Looked at him and married him,
And he squandered everything she had.

She never knew the worst, because
She died in giving birth to me,
But now she knows it all, being dead.

Great people lived and died in this house;
Magistrates, colonels, members of Parliament,
Captains and governors, and long ago
Men that had fought at Aughrim and the Boyne.
Some that had gone on government work
To London or to India came home to die,
Or came from London every spring
To look at the May-blossom in the park.
They had loved the trees that he cut down
To pay what he had lost at cards
Or spent on horses, drink and women;
Had loved the house, had loved all
The intricate passages of the house,
But he killed the house; to kill a house
Where great men grew up, married, died,
I here declare a capital offence.

BOY My God, but you had luck. Grand clothes,
And maybe a grand horse to ride.

OLD MAN That he might keep me upon his level
He never sent me to school, but some
Half-loved me for my half of her,
A gamekeeper's wife taught me to read,
A Catholic curate taught me Latin.
There were old books and books made fine
By eighteenth century French binding, books
Modern and ancient, books by the ton.

BOY What education have you given me?

55

OLD MAN I gave the education that befits
A bastard that a peddlar got
Upon a tinker's daughter in a ditch.

When I had come into my sixteenth year
My father burned down the house when drunk.

BOY But that is my age, sixteen years old.
At the Puck Fair

OLD MAN And everything was burnt;
Books, library, all were burnt.

BOY Is what I have heard upon the road the truth,
That you killed him in the burning house?

OLD MAN There's nobody here but our two selves?

BOY Nobody, Father.

OLD MAN I stuck him with a knife,
That knife that cuts my dinner now,
And after that I left him in the fire;
They dragged him out, somebody saw
The knife-wound but could not be certain
Because the body was all black and charred.
Then some that were his drunken friends
Swore they would put me upon trial,
Spoke of quarrels, a threat I had made.
The gamekeeper gave me some old clothes,
I ran away, worked here and there
Till I became a pedlar on the roads,
No good trade, but good enough
Because I am my father's son,
Because of what I did or may do.

Listen to the hoof beats! Listen, listen!

BOY I cannot hear a sound.

5

56

OLD MAN Beat! Beat!
This night is the anniversary
Of my mother's wedding night,
Or of the night wherein I was begotten.
My father is riding from the public house
A whiskey bottle under his arm.

(a window is lit, showing a young girl)

Look at the window; she stands there
Listening, the servants are all in bed,
She is alone, he has stayed late
Bragging and drinking in the public house.

BOY There's nothing ~~in the window, all there is black,~~ but an empty gap in the wall.
You have made it up. No, you are mad!
You are getting madder every day.

OLD MAN It's louder now because he rides
Upon a gravelled avenue
All grass today. The hoof beats stops,
He has gone to the other side of the house
To put the horse up. ~~All that is hidden~~
~~But I can see it all in the mind.~~ gone to the stable
She has gone down to open the door.
This night she is no better than her man
And does not mind that he is half drunk,
She is mad about him. They mount the stairs
She brings him into her own chamber. ~~Now~~
Range The window is dimly lit again
~~Because she has put the candle upon the table~~
~~And the passage door is open; now~~
~~That door is shut and the window dark.~~

O do not let him touch you! It is not true
That drunken men cannot beget
And if he touch he must beget
And you must bear his murderer.

Deaf! Both deaf! If I shoud throw
A stick or a stone they would not hear;
And that's a proof my wits are out.
But here's a problem: she must live

And that is The marriage chamber now

57

OLD MAN: Through everything in exact detail,
 Driven to it by remorse, and yet
Can she renew the sexual act
And find no pleasure in it, and if not
I pleasure and remorse must both be there
Which is the greater?
 I lack schooling.
Go fetch Tertullian; he and I
Will ravel all that problem out
Whilst those two lie upon the mattress
Begetting me.
 Come back! Come back!
And so you thought to slip away,
My bag of money between your fingers,
And that I could not talk and see!

You have been rummaging in the pack.

(<u>The light in the window has faded out</u>)

BOY: You never gave me a share.

OLD MAN: And had I given it, young as you are
You would have spent it upon drink.

BOY: What if I did? I had a right
To get my share and spend it as I chose.

OLD MAN: Give me that bag and no more words.

BOY: ~~[illegible]~~ I will not.

OLD MAN: I can change that song.

(<u>They struggle for the bag. In the struggle it drops, scattering the money. The old man staggers but does not fall. They stand looking at each other</u>)

BOY: What if I killed you? You killed my grand-dad.
Because you were young and he was old.
Now I am young and you are old.

(<u>window is lit up, a man is seening pouring whiskey into a glass.</u>)

58

OLD MAN (staring at window) ~~there~~
Better looking, ~~though~~ sixteen years -

BOY: What are you muttering?

OLD MAN: Younger - and yet
She should have known he was not ~~of~~ her kind.

BOY: What are you saying? Out with it!

(Old Man points to window.)

BOY: My God! The window is lit up
And somebody stands there, although
The floorboards are all burnt away.

OLD MAN: The window is lit up because my father
Has come to find a glass for his whiskey.
He leans there like some tired beast.

BOY: A dead, living, murdered man ~~[illegible]~~!

OLD MAN Then the bride sleep fell upon Adam;
Where did I read those words?
And yet
There's nothing leaning in the window
But the impression upon my mother's mind,
Being dead she is alone in her remorse.

BOY: A body that was a bundle of old bones
Before I was born. Horrible! Horrible!

(he covers his eyes)

OLD MAN: That beast there would know nothing, being nothing,
If I should kill a man under the window,
He would not even turn his head.

(he stabs the BOY)

My father and my son on the same jack-knife!
That finishes - there - there - there -

(he stabs again and again. The window grows dark.)

59

OLD MAN: "Hush-a-bye baby, thy father's a knight,
Thy mother a lady, lovely and bright."

No, that is something that I read in a book
And if I sing it must be to my mother,
And I lack rhyme.

(the stage has grown dark except where the tree stands in white light)

Study that tree.
It stands there like a purified soul,
All cold, sweet, glistening light.
Dear mother, the window is dark again
But you are in the light because
I finished all that consequence.
I killed that lad for he was growing up,
He would soon take some woman's fancy,
Beget, and pass pollution on.
I am a wretched foul old man
And therefore harmless when I have stuck
This old jack knife into a sod
And pulled it out all bright again,
And picked up all the money that he dropped
I'll to a distant place, and there
Tell my old jokes among new men.

(he cleans the knife and begins to pick up money)

Hoof beats! Dear God
How quickly it returns - beat - beat -

Her mind cannot hold up that dream.
Twice a murderer and all for nothing,
And she must animate that dead night
Not once but many times!
O God!
Release my mother's soul from its dream!
Mankind can do no more. Appease
The misery of the living and the remorse of
the dead.

First Set of the Longford Page Proofs

PURGATORY

(A ruined house and a bare tree in the background).

Boy: Half door, hall door
Hither and thither day and night
Hill or hollow, shouldering this pack.
Hearing you talk.

Old Man: Study that house.
I think about its jokes and stories;
I try to remember what the butler
Said to a drunken gamekeeper
In mid-October, but I cannot,
If I cannot, none living can.
Where are the jokes and stories of a house,
Its threshold gone to patch a pig-stye?

Boy: So you have come this path before?

Old Man: The moonlight falls upon the path,
The shadow of a cloud upon the house
And that's symbolical; study that tree,
What is it like?

Boy: A silly old man.

Old Man: It's like—no matter what it's like.
I saw it a year ago stripped bare as now,

34 ON THE BOILER 87

I saw it fifty years ago
Before the thunder-bolt had riven it,
Green leaves, ripe leaves, leaves thick as butter,
Fat, greasy life. Stand there and look,
Because there is somebody in that house.

(The BOY puts down pack and stands in the doorway)

Boy: There's nobody here.

Old Man: There's somebody there.

Boy: The floor is gone, the windows gone,
And where there should be roof there's sky,
And here's a bit of an egg-shell thrown
Out of a jackdaw's nest.

Old Man: But there are some
That do not care what's gone what's left,
The souls in Purgatory that come back
To habitations and familiar spots.

Boy: Your wits are out again.

Old Man: Re-live
Their transgressions, and that not once
But many times, they know at last
The consequence of those transgressions
Whether upon others, or upon themselves;
Upon others, others may bring help
For when the consequence is at an end
The dream must end; upon themselves
There is no help but in themselves
And in the mercy of God.

Boy: I have had enough!
Talk to the jackdaws, if talk you must.

Old Man: Stop! Sit there upon that stone.
That is the house where I was born.

Boy: The big old house that was burnt down?

Old Man: My mother that was your grand-dam owned it,
This scenery and this countryside,

~~ON THE BOILER~~ 35

Kennel and stable, horse and hound—

She had a horse at the Curragh, and there met
My father, a groom in a training stable;
Looked at him and married him.
Her mother never spoke to her again,
And she did right.

~~**Boy:**~~ What's right and wrong?
My grand-dad got the girl and the money.

Old Man: Looked at him and married him,
And he squandered everything she had.

She never knew the worst, because
She died in giving birth to me,
But now she knows it all, being dead.

Great people lived and died in this house;
Magistrates, colonels, members of Parliament,
Captains and Governors, and long ago
Men that had fought at Aughrim and the Boyne.
Some that had gone on government work
To London or to India came home to die,
Or came from London every spring
To look at the May-blossom in the park.
They had loved the trees that he cut down
To pay what he had lost at cards
Or spent on horses, drink and women;
Had loved the house, had loved all
The intricate passages of the house,
But he killed the house; to kill a house
Where great men grew up, married, died,
I here declare a capital offence.

Boy: My God, but you had luck. Grand clothes,
And maybe a grand horse to ride.

Old Man: That he might keep me upon his level
He never sent me to school, but some
Half-loved me for my half of her,
A gamekeeper's wife taught me to read,
A Catholic curate taught me Latin.

36 ON THE BOILER

There were old books and books made fine
By eighteenth century French binding, books
Modern and ancient, books by the ton.

Boy: What education have you given me?

Old Man: I gave the education that befits
A bastard that a peddlar got
Upon a tinker's daughter in a ditch.

When I had come to sixteen years old
My father burned down the house when drunk.

Boy: But that is my age, sixteen years old.
At the Puck Fair.

Old Man: And everything was burnt;
Books, library, all were burnt.

Boy: Is what I have heard upon the road the truth,
That you killed him in the burning house?

Old Man: There's nobody here but our two selves?

Boy: Nobody, Father.

Old Man: I stuck him with a knife,

That knife that cuts my dinner now,
And after that I left him in the fire;
They dragged him out, somebody saw
The knife-wound but could not be certain
Because the body was all black and charred.
Then some that were his drunken friends
Swore they would put me upon trial,
Spoke of quarrels, a threat I had made.
The gamekeeper gave me some old clothes,
I ran away, worked here and there
Till I became a pedlar on the roads,
No good trade, but good enough
Because I am my father's son,
Because of what I did or may do.

Listen to the hoof beats! Listen, listen!

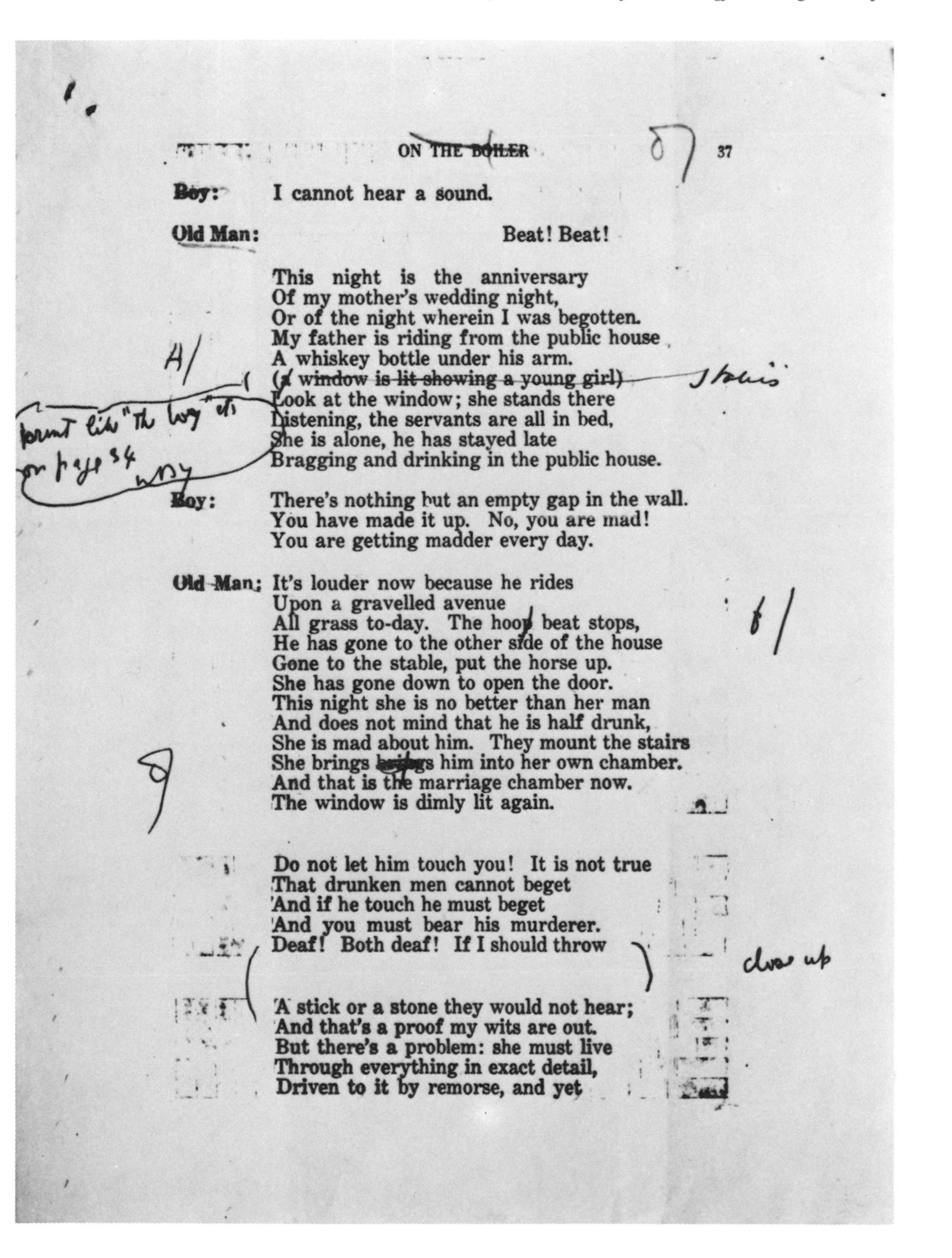

ON THE BOILER 37

Boy: I cannot hear a sound.

Old Man: Beat! Beat!

This night is the anniversary
Of my mother's wedding night,
Or of the night wherein I was begotten.
My father is riding from the public house
A whiskey bottle under his arm.
(A window is lit showing a young girl)
Look at the window; she stands there
Listening, the servants are all in bed,
She is alone, he has stayed late
Bragging and drinking in the public house.

Boy: There's nothing but an empty gap in the wall.
You have made it up. No, you are mad!
You are getting madder every day.

Old Man: It's louder now because he rides
Upon a gravelled avenue
All grass to-day. The hoop beat stops,
He has gone to the other side of the house
Gone to the stable, put the horse up.
She has gone down to open the door.
This night she is no better than her man
And does not mind that he is half drunk,
She is mad about him. They mount the stairs
She brings brings him into her own chamber.
And that is the marriage chamber now.
The window is dimly lit again.

Do not let him touch you! It is not true
That drunken men cannot beget
And if he touch he must beget
And you must bear his murderer.
Deaf! Both deaf! If I should throw

A stick or a stone they would not hear;
And that's a proof my wits are out.
But there's a problem: she must live
Through everything in exact detail,
Driven to it by remorse, and yet

38 ON THE BOILER

Can she renew the sexual act
And find no pleasure in it, and if not
If pleasure and remorse must both be there
Which is the greater?
I lack schooling.
Go fetch Tertullian; he and I
Will ravel all that problem out
Whilst those two lie upon the mattress
Begetting me.
Come back! Come back!
And so you thought to slip away,
My bag of money between your fingers,
And that I could not talk and see!
You have been rummaging in the pack.
(The light in the window has faded out)

Boy: You never gave me my right share.

Old Man: And had I given it, young as you are
You would have spent it upon drink.

Boy: What if I did? I had a right
To get it and spend it as I chose.

Old Man: Give me that bag and no more words.

Boy: I will not.

Old Man: I will break your fingers.
(They struggle for the bag. In the struggle it drops, scattering the money. The old man staggers but does not fall. They stand looking at each other)

Boy: What if I killed you? You killed my grand-dad.
Because you were young and he was old.
Now I am young and you are old
(window is lit up, a man is seen pouring whiskey into a glass.)

Old Man: (staring at window)

Better looking, those sixteen years—

Boy: What are you muttering?

space/Italics

Italics
space

space
Italics

Italics

see "The Boy" &c
page 34
MS 34

Old Man: Younger—and yet
She should have known he was not her kind.

Boy: What are you saying? Out with it!
(Old Man points to window.)
My God! The window is lit up
And somebody stands there, although
The floorboards are all burnt away.

Old Man: The window is lit up because my father
Has come to find a glass for his whiskey.
He leans there like some tired beast.

Boy: A dead, living, murdered man.

Old Man: Then the bride sleep fell upon Adam:
Where did I read those words?
And yet
There's nothing leaning in the window
But the impression upon my mother's mind,
Being dead she is alone in her remorse.

Boy A body that was a bundle of old bones
Before I was born. Horrible! Horrible!
(He covers his eyes.)

Old Man: That beast there would know nothing, being
I fI should kill a man under the window.
He would not even turn his head.
(He stabs the BOY)
My father and my son on the same jack-knife!
That finishes—there—there—there—
(He stabs again and again. The window grows dark.)

Old Man: "Hush-a-bye baby, thy father's a knight,
Thy mother a lady, lovely and bright."
No, that is something that I read in a book
And if I sing it must be to my mother,
And I lack rhyme.
(The stage has grown dark except where the tree stands in white light).
Study that tree.

CORRECTED PROOF OF LAST PAGE OF PURGATORY

40 ON THE BOILER

It stands there like a purified soul,
All cold, sweet, glistening light.
Dear mother, the window is dark again
But you are in the light because
I finished all that consequence.
I killed that lad [illegible] growing up,
He would [illegible] woman's fancy,
Beget, and pass pollution on.
I am a wretched foul old man
And therefore harmless. When I have stuck
This old jack knife into a sod
And pulled it out all bright again,
And picked up all the money that he dropped
I'll to a distant place, and there
Tell my old jokes among new men.
(He cleans the knife and begins to pick up money.)
Hoof beats! Dear God
How quickly it returns—beat—beat—

Her mind cannot hold up that dream.
Twice a murderer and all for nothing,
And she must animate that dead night
Not once but many times!
O God
Release my mother's soul from its dream!
Mankind can do no more. Appease
The misery of the living and the remorse of
the dead.

see "The Boy" page 34 WBY